D1503071

Organizational
Change
That Works

Organizational Change That Works

How to Merge Culture and Business
Strategies for Maximum Results

Robert W. Rogers
John W. Hayden
B. Jean Ferketish
with Robert Matzen

Material from *Organizational Culture* by Frost, Moore, Louis, Lundberg, and Martin, copyright © 1985 (Sage Publications, Inc.) reprinted by permission of Sage Publications, Inc.

© Development Dimensions International, Inc., MCMXCVII.

Published by DDI Press, c/o Development Dimensions International, World Headquarters—Pittsburgh, 1225 Washington Pike, Bridgeville, Pennsylvania 15017-2838.

Manufactured in the United States of America.

Library of Congress Cataloging in Publications Data
Rogers, R.W.
    Organizational change that works: how to merge culture and business strategies for maximum results/Robert W. Rogers, John W. Hayden, B. Jean Ferketish with Robert Matzen
1. Business   2. Organizational Change
ISBN 0-9623483-5-X

10 9 8 7 6 5 4 3 2 1

CONTENTS

☆ ☆ ☆

Introduction

ome say that ongoing organizational change is a fact of life—
it won't go away, no matter how hard you try. Others accept
it as a challenge and meet it head-on with a fierce commitment to success. No matter how they look at it, the thought of launching an initiative to achieve a new vision of organizational success—and making sense out of what seems like hopeless chaos—creates heartburn and insomnia for many senior leaders. There's no mistake about it: The types of changes this initiative would require are staggering.

We wrote this book to help. For senior leaders contemplating a major change initiative, this book provides a clear map of the journey ahead, including suggestions for ensuring optimal results. For human resource and organizational dynamics consultants, this book can help guide their organizations successfully through the change process.

In a constantly evolving business environment, enlightened leaders understand the need to redirect their organizations—to pay attention to customer retention as well as return on investment, to focus on process improvements and reengineering as well as productivity, and to meet employee needs for long-term opportunities rather than just satisfy short-term financial goals.

Good leaders have handled business evolution through reengineering, mergers and acquisitions, empowerment, and competency-based systems. They've stressed total quality; they've stressed high-performance teams. The business initiatives they've undertaken, all of which fall under the organizational change umbrella, require *people* to adapt to the changes required to assure organizational success. These leaders understand that through it all, there is a constant that cannot be taken for granted: *the workforce*. People make the changes. People cope with the chaos. People make or break organizations.

The drivers of change vary with the industry. Mergers and acquisitions drive change in banking and health care.

Deregulation drives change for utilities. Cost containment drives change in the public sector. And as these drivers shift, so does the nature of the workforce. People have come out of the past decade of leveraged buy-outs and downsizing with different views about "company loyalty," and organizations can no longer offer job security in exchange for that loyalty.

The current equation is simple: Organizations that don't *show* loyalty don't *earn* loyalty. In these organizations employees won't sacrifice quality of life for promotions and financial rewards. Surveys back that up—job security no longer tops the list of what people want from their jobs. They now prioritize autonomy, involvement, challenge, and personal growth above the once-precious job security.

Leaders must prepare organizations to respond to external business drivers and, at the same time, consider employees' revised priorities and expectations—the internal drivers of change. It's no easy task, and enlightened leaders realize that taking on that task means organizational change of some kind. These leaders also understand that change of any magnitude consumes time, money, and resources, and more often than not, it fails. Most senior leaders also know why their change efforts fail. Just ask one, and you'll hear, "We failed because it was too difficult to change our culture."

In this context what exactly does *culture* mean? Organizational culture is the behavior of all the *people* in the organization. That behavior must align with and be directed toward achieving the business strategy. In fact, most change efforts fail because *people* are not involved in the change, and consequently they're not committed to forging a new future.

When this *human* side of the change process fails, the entire effort collapses. Benjamin Franklin captured it quite succinctly: "We must hang together or we will most assuredly hang separately." What helps people "hang together"? What gives them the direction they need in time of turmoil? The answer is values. Values serve as the motivation and the glue for people to work together toward a common goal.

Unfortunately, in most change interventions leaders press for quick solutions and, consequently, do not allow for the time and effort it takes to involve people—an approach that's critical to making the change work. The reason, we find, is that leaders often consider the method for involving people in organizational change to be some great mystery or scientific formula. It's not. It's simply a process for directing organizations toward a desired destination of success. *Organizational Change That Works* is based on a process model that merges culture and business strategies, allowing the people in an organization to help reinvent its destiny. This strategy works at the beginning of an organizational change effort or at any point along this fundamentally important journey into the future.

Advocating a *value-driven* approach to organizational change that addresses the culture does not ignore bottom-line results. The approach and process we propose actually integrate the business side with the human side to produce an accurate, detailed map for change. This map helps organizations in three ways. First, it provides a focus for channeling workforce energy. Second, it achieves effective change by involving others. Finally, it aligns key organizational processes and systems.

Involving people in the change effort, whether they contribute ideas, align systems, or actually design the change, paves the way for a smoother transition. Employee involvement can also mean increased flexibility and speed in addressing problems and issues, improved responsiveness to customers and market opportunities, reduced cycle time, innovation, productivity, continuous improvement, and financial success.

Wherever you are or choose to go on the quest to realize your organization's vision of success, it's critical to keep in mind that organizations are people, and it's our nature as human beings to resist change. However, we also are more likely to accept and commit to change if we see a brighter future, if we have a say in the change process, and if we understand our role in the quest for change that really works.

Organizational Change That Works is meant to be a simple, nonacademic reference tool—a map like any other, which you can open up to find out where you are and where you need to go. Our value-driven change process is based on years of experience at Development Dimensions International (DDI), dealing with hundreds of organizations undergoing change. The process, therefore, is designed to help set a course for change that can be tailored to any organizational situation. Its bottom line is improved results predicated on shifts in workplace behavior—starting at the top.

To connect the reader with the possibilities inherent in organizational change, we refer occasionally to turning a vision—a leader's challenge to explore new frontiers—into reality. This type of quest once rallied a large group of people toward a common direction, culminating in the most memorable voyage of the twentieth century: Apollo 11's mission to the lunar surface. Our repeated allusion to this example hopefully will remind us all that if a trip to the moon can be accomplished, so can organizational change.

Let's launch a journey into a new century with a look at value-driven change in theory and in fact, as seen through the eyes of successful organizations. What beckons is a stronger, more productive workplace for you and your associates—a workplace that can withstand and succeed in the turbulence of a constantly evolving business world.

Bob Rogers

John Hayden

Jean Ferketish

Robert Matzen

March 1997

CHAPTER 1

ORGANIZATIONS AT THE CROSSROADS

Tomorrow's business success stories will feature organizations that put as much time and effort into their culture strategies as they do their business strategies. This is not a psychic prediction; it is a practical interpretation of a business world in which organizations are placing increasing emphasis on their cultures.

The media spotlights success stories of dynamic leaders building solid organizations—companies now flooded with resumes from prospective employees who want to participate in the culture as well as the success. It all seems so simplistic from the outside. From the inside it's not nearly so effortless. Leaders in these successful organizations follow a plan, using skills and abilities—every day—that they've gleaned from the hardships of reaching their dreamed-of heights.

The media is drawn to companies whose quests for success already are years old. And, it's only the media spotlight that makes the public take notice. Most people never see the struggle, the pain, the soul searching, the courage, or the work that precedes the lofty heights of success. All are part of the success story because change initiatives commonly begin at a point in an organization's history when its leaders realize that what worked in the past won't work in the future, that "business as usual" won't drive future success, that the market is evolving, that technology is reinventing business, that the rules have changed, that customers aren't happy, that productivity is sliding, that the bottom line isn't good—and will get worse, and that the competition is overrunning them. These are the times when leaders say what they have always said: "We've got to *do something*."

In May 1961 competition overran the United States government. In the midst of the Cold War between superpowers, in an age when the Soviet satellite Sputnik had sent panic through the U.S. and its allies, an astronaut named Yuri Gagarin became the first man to orbit the earth. This stunning achievement caught a fledgling organization—NASA—flat-footed.

The implications were staggering. At a time when the U.S. and the U.S.S.R. wrestled for the control of nations, the most powerful country would attract support. And space superiority meant power. How would the U.S. respond? A space program existed, but it was a maelstrom of success and failure—of successful test flights and of rockets exploding on the launch pad. The various branches of the military had fought like street gangs over turf and technology. And now the United States reeled as Yuri Gagarin received the accolades of the world.

It can happen to any organization. It happens to most at one time or another. Leaders don't always know how they got there. It seems like the competition just snuck up on them. But however they arrived at this situation, they find themselves sitting at the crossroads of success and failure. The roads aren't labeled, so leaders hesitate, pondering which way to go.

Miller Brewing Company sat at this intersection in the '80s. With more than $4 billion in yearly sales, Miller maintained a position as number two in U.S. brewing. To meet growing demand for its products, Miller began building a $410 million plant in Trenton, Ohio, in 1981. But by its completion in 1983, beer sales had tailed off, and Miller's expansion plans fell through. The plant sat idle, stunning the area north of Cincinnati, which had counted on more than a thousand new jobs.

As 1990 approached, regional beers and microbreweries appeared, and competition within the beer industry became fierce. Miller wanted nothing more than to remain competitive by boosting production and utilizing that idle plant in Ohio. But how?

NIBCO Incorporated, a leading manufacturer of industrial pipe valves and fittings, found itself at the same intersection in 1993. One of its facilities sprawled over two city blocks, with departmentalized areas for assembly, machining, and molding. It took six weeks to go from raw material to finished goods. Thirty-one associates touched the product as it progressed through its laborious cycle, traveling 2,600 feet—a half mile.

NIBCO Administrative Coordinator Jon Woodworth describes the plant, with its physical layout limitations and functional silos. "The production area had its own turf. So did Machining and Molding. Each of these areas was very particular about what happened in the operation. Associates were very limited in the scope of their jobs. Their thinking was, 'If my job has these four responsibilities, that's all I can do. If I try to do something else, I'm stepping on somebody else's turf or their job functions.' This thinking stretched even to preventive maintenance-type things."

The NIBCO plant also experienced the pain of inconstant ownership. It changed hands three times in 20 years. Daily, leaders coped with the culture and the processes of companies long gone. The plant layout and process had evolved slowly and unplanned, from owner to owner, and the lead time and scrap rates reflected it. Woodworth gives a typical example of process inefficiency. "You might mold 3,000 parts, send them to Machining, and the first 5 don't fit on the machine. All of a sudden, you're scrapping 3,000 parts."

How long can a manufacturing organization survive when it scraps 3,000 parts at a time? As 1993 gave way to 1994, NIBCO sat at the crossroads.

The Buick Motor Division of General Motors Corporation had

reached the same intersection for entirely different reasons. The '80s had seen American auto manufacturers strive to equal the quality levels of foreign manufacturers, such as Honda and Toyota. In the '90s increased quality made American automakers viable players in the game, whereupon they learned that the global stakes had been raised to include customer retention and loyalty.

Despite Buick's efforts in the field of quality, customer satisfaction rates of 93 to 96 percent still didn't ensure customer retention and profitability. These numbers reflected that a significant number of Buick owners were choosing not to come back. For Buick to remain an industry leader, it needed to continuously sharpen its focus on eliciting customer loyalty. Buick's leaders knew they needed to bring to life their corporatewide vision, *Customer Care That Says You're Family.* There Buick sat—at the crossroads.

Blue Cross and Blue Shield® of Montana also sat at the crossroads. Different organization, same basic problems. In 1993 the company was doing just fine. In business for 50 years, its health care plans provided protection for a quarter of a million Montanans. The company is measured on a Blue Cross/Blue Shield National Management Information Standards scale, obligating it to provide the highest possible standard of service in 10 service categories (claims timeliness, claims accuracy, accuracy of information given, and so on).

But how could the company provide the highest service if cumbersome procedures and nonaligned systems then in place did nothing but hold it back? For example, the new group-enrollment process identified 157 steps. (Of these steps, 50 are now targeted for elimination, and the process will eventually be reduced to 10 major service steps.) The customer service and adjustments departments, located in different buildings, required days to transfer information and make the most minor account changes or corrections.

Jane DeLong, vice president of Corporate Resources and Quality Management, described the system as it related to simple customer calls about eligibility and claims status: "What we would do is fill out a form and put it in the interoffice mail and send it across the street to our adjustments department. Then they'd make the adjustment and send it back across the street, and then the person would call the customer about three days later—it could even be a week." These were procedures that evolved because of rapid growth. But in a world giving ever greater scrutiny to service and service organizations, could Blue Cross and Blue Shield of Montana afford to maintain this status quo?

Its President and Chief Executive Officer Alan F. Cain and senior management envisioned a better way of doing things. Cain believes, "A person should be able to buy a product that will respond when that person needs medical services in such a way that very high-quality services are delivered at a very low cost with a lot less hassle than we have now." But how does a 50-year-old health-care insurer transform into this service-oriented entity?

The insurance industry in general has felt the shock waves of economics and competition. Monolithic institutions built around inflexible management and narrowly defined jobs have taken hit after hit in the economic and competitive arenas of the past decade. Processes have become so ingrained in these institutions that people can perform their single-task jobs by rote. They answer questions like, "Why does it take a week to adjust a claim?" by saying, "Because that's the system." They want to put in their time. They want to go home. Better jobs provide nice daydreams, but just speculating about what it might take to achieve such a paradise makes the mind reel. The environment is command and control, with workers driven by job descriptions, performance evaluations, and compensation. They play it safe, take no risks, and hope to keep their jobs. Their cultures beg a change; their bottom lines scream it.

The need for change is global. Figure 1, from a 1996 report by David Ulrich and Robert Eichinger of The Human Resource Planning Society (HRPS), represents results of a recent survey taken by the society. The survey sought input from thought leaders throughout North America and Europe about business conditions and corresponding human resource implications. One part of the survey centered on competitive challenges facing organizations in the future. The questions asked in this section were, "To what extent do you see the following as challenges facing organizations?" and "How well do you see organizations dealing with these issues?" Responses were scaled from 1 (low) to 5 (high).

To what extent do you see the following as challenges facing organizations?			Issue	How well do you see organizations dealing with these issues?		
Overall	U.S.	Europe		Overall	U.S.	Europe
4.53	4.46	4.64	Creating an adaptive culture with a capacity for rapid change.	2.49	2.36	2.71
4.45	4.50	4.36	Becoming a more effective global competitor.	2.95	2.92	3.00
4.38	4.62	3.93	Attracting, developing, and retaining top talent; creating the leadership bench.	3.08	3.12	3.00
4.13	4.27	3.86	Building and operating a more effective customer responsive organization.	3.33	3.27	3.43
3.87	3.80	4.00	Increasing innovation.	2.82	2.84	2.79
3.82	3.73	4.00	Being a low-cost or best-price/value provider.	3.49	3.35	3.77
3.73	3.69	3.79	Transitioning from profit through cost cutting to profit by revenue growth.	2.50	2.31	2.86
3.68	3.71	3.64	Increasing speed.	3.15	3.12	3.21
3.65	3.69	3.57	Taking advantage of new information technology.	3.15	3.16	3.14
3.28	3.19	3.43	Reengineering all work processes.	2.80	2.92	2.57

Figure 1. Competitive Challenges from The Human Resource Planning Society SOTA 96, Round II Report by David Ulrich and Robert Eichinger, 1996. Adapted with permission.

As stated in the report, the resulting data encompass "the mean scores for the overall sample, the United States, and European thought leaders." These results reveal a statistical gap. The scores in the right column—how well organizations are meeting competitive challenges—are lower than those in the left column—representing the challenges themselves. Also, according to the findings, "the largest numerical gaps between the challenge and the response have to do with creating an adaptive culture with the capacity for rapid change, being a global competitor, and attracting and developing talent."

The HRPS report found that it is essential for future business successes to create "adaptable and changeable cultures that are . . . more global in scope and reach, with a more critical need for developing leadership talent." The authors believe that "HR practices and professionals need to consider getting better at (1) creating cultures that can change more rapidly and (2) creating truly global enterprises." Surveys such as this one highlight the critical role of culture in an organization's response to the challenges of tomorrow's business world.

The companies cited in this chapter were forced to respond to specific and critical business challenges. Miller Brewing Company had spent years doing things a certain way, emphasizing equipment and facilities. NIBCO had lived too long with inefficient processes. Buick was good with customers—and wanted to be better. Blue Cross and Blue Shield of Montana had become focused on complex departmental systems.

Throughout the business world organizations can become sluggish. Rumors circulate that heads will roll or a buyout is near or layoffs are around the corner. Every senior leader has read about it. Most worry about it. And each day brings new pressures, new competition, new technology, and new regulations. And leaders think to themselves, "We have to change, and we have to do it soon." The quest begins.

CHAPTER 2

INTEGRATION OF CULTURE AND BUSINESS STRATEGIES

☆ ☆ ☆

NIBCO opened a new plant in Charlestown, Indiana, in 1996. This facility, 187,000 square feet in size, experiences a cycle time of two weeks rather than the previous six. At the new plant various production measures improved dramatically over those at other NIBCO facilities. The product there travels 530 feet during manufacturing instead of a half mile and is handled by 14 associates rather than 31. When a product moves from an injection molding machine to a lathe, dimensions are checked immediately, and if incorrect, the operation scraps a handful of parts, not 3,000—the astronomical former scrap statistic.

For Jon Woodworth, Charlestown's environment represents a significant departure from the cultures at other NIBCO manufacturing facilities: "I would say the old culture drove the new culture, from the sheer fact that we wanted a big change. When they go through orientation, we tell all of our associates from the other facility to drop off their baggage when they come in. There are some things we did in the other facility that were good, but for the most part, we want to hear new ideas, fresh ideas, and don't want to hear, 'Do it a certain way just because we've always done it that way.' We're trying to create a new environment."

Quality and production measures back up the decision of senior leadership to take a new direction at NIBCO. A heightened awareness of the importance of quality in the parts produced has motivated workers to conduct more spot inspections. When necessary, Charlestown employees are taking the responsibility to say, "If I were the customer, I don't think I would want to buy this product." As a result, there is an improved awareness for quality production. For NIBCO it's only the beginning. A second plant, this one in Goshen, Indiana, has embarked on a similar change effort, and two others will begin a culture change soon, affecting a total of 1,500 employees.

The Miller Brewing Company plant in Trenton, Ohio, employs 440 people. With base wages and overtime Miller technicians earn as much as $57,000 per year, which is a boon to the local economy. Relations between Miller and the representative union, the United Auto Workers, are cordial. The Trenton plant produces a barrel of beer in 30 percent less time than other Miller breweries, and labor costs also have been reduced by 30 percent. Plant efficiency made it attractive to brew multiple brands at Trenton. The plant, originally projected to produce 5 brands, now brews 18.

The people at Miller work hard; they cram training in around long hours. But something special is visible at Trenton—a plantwide dedication to excellence and, more importantly, an excitement that things are going well.

Eighteen months after making the decision to embark on the change quest, Buick rolled out a culture change to more than 25,000 dealership employees. While results varied among the 500 dealerships, reports showed an 18 percent increase in customer loyalty.

The reports also reflected a greater sensitivity in dealing with difficult customers; an improved response to customer phone calls; a number of internal improvements, such as better intradepartmental communication; and a heightened appreciation of coworkers' differences and contributions. Dealers use customer appreciation days to establish and maintain solid relationships with their customers, and they encourage employee satisfaction by listening and responding to their problems and ideas. Communication has improved dramatically, both internally among employees and externally with customers.

Changes at Blue Cross and Blue Shield of Montana are no less dramatic. Gone are many of the silos that once contained and limited the operation. Many more will be going away soon, and the measurable results are amazing. Says Jane DeLong, "About four months ago our Blue Cross/Blue Shield National Management Information Standards scores were hovering around 75. Four months later they're up into the 95s, and the top scores are about 100."

In three years the organization has undergone sweeping changes and converted to high-performance teams. "You can really feel the whole culture moving ahead," says DeLong, "and we have tons left to do. We have to look at some of the support areas—How are they going to evolve? How are they going to change? There is still some resistance, especially when you're actually looking at a process that crosses divisional lines. You have people that have definitely bought into the fact that they know this is where we're going, this is what we're going to do, so I'd better get with the action."

How did NIBCO improve its manufacturing process so dramatically? How did Miller successfully open that idle plant? How did Buick increase customer loyalty? How did Blue Cross and Blue Shield of Montana position itself to meet customer needs?

Change and the Workforce

In each of these organizations, senior leadership initiated a change effort. They saw their companies' shortcomings and developed a vision of what they wanted the business to be, to look like, to represent. Then they began the quest to achieve that vision. They generated ideas that grew into convictions. The new vision in each organization led to an examination of processes and systems with the purpose of refocusing the organization on customer needs and wants.

These events mirror the space race that began with Sputnik and Yuri Gagarin and a flat-footed United States and ended less than eight years later, on July 20, 1969, when astronauts Neil Armstrong and Buzz Aldrin landed on the lunar surface and then returned safely to earth.

The story of the U.S. space effort during this eight-year time period is epic in scope. It involves not merely the success of the Apollo 11 mission, but more fundamentally the presidential mandate to explore new frontiers and put a man on the moon. It was a mandate that required the commitment of everyone in NASA. And it succeeded.

The NASA example becomes relevant because no one person or handful of people could have accomplished a lunar landing. It required everyone in the organization to pitch in and help. Without them, the effort would have failed. How those people approached their jobs and how they related to one another and to people outside the organization helped to determine whether they would reach the dreamed-of future.

Of course, organizational visions don't always revolve around something as sweeping as a call to explore new frontiers in outer space. Organizational change efforts don't always require the alignment of civilian and government agencies, not to mention scores of subcontractors. All organizational change initiatives *do*, however, have people as a common element. People in the workforce effect change; change affects the people in the workforce.

Back in the days when NASA was reaching for the moon, workers were valued only for their outputs. This view has changed with the increasing exploration of the concepts of work, work processes, and culture. Today, workers—and the commitment they bring with them to work every day—are perceived as vital to achieving business results, and organizational culture is believed to be the key to securing that all-important commitment.

Organizational culture is the sum of all the behaviors of all the people in an organization. It encompasses their interactions within the organization and with external customers as they go about company business. It includes everything from official company policy to the briefest of individual interactions. The concept of organizational culture has been the subject of numerous books, articles, and studies that attest to the business world's changing perception of culture.

In the past decade evidence has mounted connecting organizational culture and realities such as profit and profitability. *Organizational Culture* (1986) by Frost, Moore, Louis, Lundberg, and Martin was one of many studies of the subject. In it one of the authors, Meryl Reis Louis, tied workplace culture with productivity and its effect on profitability. Further, she challenged what she described as the long-held, "old" theory—that culture designed exclusively for and within the top echelon of an organization would sink downward and permeate the workplace. In other words, leadership behaviors exhibited in the executive suites would inspire the workforce from afar.

This theory did not prove correct. Instead, subcultures filled the void left by a lack of culture guidance from the top. This sparked Louis' interest in studying these subcultures to see if they could be guided or designed. "It . . . also has raised issues," she said, "about how feasible it is to alter the culture of an organizational unit and what is involved in doing so—namely, the means of revitalizing cultures and of harnessing subcultures to larger corporate aims and cultures" (p. 86).

Louis forms the foundation of a case for the importance of organizational culture by concluding, "There is solid documentation that overlooking organizational culture has impeded efforts to change organizational functioning. Examination of past failures in organizational development efforts points to the role of culture as a critical force to be considered in effecting change" (p. 86).

In the book, *Corporate Culture and Performance* (1992), John Kotter and James Heskett quantified the impact of a strong organizational culture on financial performance. Their research suggests that an organizational report card contains two major components: financial results and culture results. While finance would obviously seem to be the dominant statistic, cultural characteristics can take precedence on the report card because culture enables an organization to achieve its financial objectives. This is a key point: *Organizational culture enables financial objectives to be achieved.*

Kotter and Heskett charted the impact of organizational culture on long-term economic performance. Their findings showed that companies with a culture that focused on strong

	Average for 12 Firms with Performance-Enhancing Cultures (%)	Average for 20 Firms without Performance-Enhancing Cultures (%)
Revenue Growth	682	166
Employment Growth	282	36
Stock Price Growth	901	74
Tax Base (Net Income) Growth	756	1

Figure 2. The Economics and Social Costs of Low-Performance Cultures (1977–1988). Reprinted with the permission of The Free Press, a division of Simon & Schuster, from *Corporate Culture and Performance* (p. 78) by John P. Kotter and James L. Heskett. Copyright © 1992 by Kotter Associates, Inc., and James L. Heskett.

leadership, customers, stockholders, and employees performed at dramatically higher levels than those without these features. Figure 2 presents the surprising summary of their findings over an 11-year period.

Further evidence of the impact of an organization's culture on its long-term economic performance comes from authors David L. Ross and James A. Benson, who studied the Sundstrand Corporation, a *Fortune* 500 company (1995). Sundstrand, an aerospace government contractor with a culture that *seemed* to be ethical, was really driven by intense competitive pressure to rack up profits while still presenting attractive deals to the government. This led to an *anything goes* environment. An ambiguous set of governmental standards also contributed to Sunstrand's lean toward unethical conduct. Unpunished ethics violations eventually became standard practice and led to government charges of billing irregularities, cost overruns, and tax abuse.

Ross and Benson point out that Sunstrand's lack of ethics within the culture caused an initial denial of responsibility.

Threatened with debarment from future Defense Department contracts, top management finally decided to pay the fines and admit to violations—but they did not address underlying culture problems. A companywide morale crisis ensued because the workforce felt disconnected from leadership, and company ethics were at odds with the personal ethics of many employees.

With the culture floundering, the company realized its only way out was to renew the culture link to ethical awareness. Sundstrand appointed a new CEO who clearly valued ethics above profit and communicated this value to the workforce in official communications as well as at company functions. Next, the company created two new positions: vice president for contracts and compliance and director of business conduct and ethics. The former would be accountable for financial ethics; the latter would retrain the entire workforce in ethical conduct. The result: Sundstrand not only avoided debarment but created high morale and an environment of trust. And most significant, profit margins doubled from 7 percent prior to the scandal to 14 percent following the culture change.

Another study, this one focusing on market-oriented cultures in service firms, hypothesizes a link between organizational marketing culture and marketing effectiveness. Although what author Cynthia Webster describes as a "marketing culture" might not be appropriate for every organization, the study still demonstrates the strength that a culture can bring to a business strategy. According to Webster (1995):

> Marketing culture is that component of a firm's overall culture that refers to the pattern of shared values and beliefs that help employees understand and "feel" the marketing function and thereby provides them with norms for behavior in the firm. It refers to the importance the firm as a whole places on marketing and to the way in which marketing activities are executed in the firm. (paragraph 6)

As defined by the author, marketing effectiveness encompasses closeness to the customer, external customer orientation, knowledge of the market and which sections to serve, and the design of a profitable strategy. Webster concludes:

The current research indicates that marketing culture, given its relationship to profitability and marketing effectiveness, may be a key ingredient for success. Companies that develop, maintain, and promote a strong marketing culture in their firms should find themselves stronger in operational efficiency, customer satisfaction, etc., than firms that ignore such a culture. (paragraph 41)

All these studies and many others point to the impact of culture—an organization's *personality*—on business strategy. When leaders create a culture strategy and integrate it with a business strategy, they greatly increase their chances of success.

Business Strategy Defined

Senior leaders are responsible for developing a long-term plan that addresses the major business concerns of the organization. This business strategy guides their decisions about the organization's markets, the types of products and services it will offer, its relationship with customers, and the distribution channels used to reach those customers. The desired result is achieving financial objectives.

Culture Strategy Defined

A culture strategy is a long-term plan for maximizing the human assets (people) of an organization and living a set of commonly shared beliefs. It defines the type of culture an organization wants to achieve. Will it be customer oriented? A culture driven by innovation? A culture that prizes quality above all else?

In the context of such a strategy, the workforce is seen as an asset rather than an expense. The culture-strategy goal is to maximize people's contributions by harnessing their convictions, enthusiasm, and passion in support of the business strategy.

Integrating the Strategies

In too many organizations senior leaders give attention to business strategy at the expense of culture. In these organizations there is no culture strategy. Leaders give culture management a quick glance, often relegating it to the human resources department. The work of Louis, Kotter, and others shows the folly of this approach.

A well-thought-out business strategy must be integrated with a culture strategy that has been given just as much consideration. The studies cited provide overwhelming evidence that leaders should focus as much on retaining employees as they do on retaining customers, and as much on employee job satisfaction as on the return on assets. Organizations that put as much time and effort into culture strategies as they do business strategies have always been winners, and this will not change.

Aligning Processes and Systems to Support Integration

To ensure success, organizational processes and systems must be aligned to support the culture strategy as well as the business strategy. *Processes* are the sequence of activities and procedures that people follow to accomplish work. *Systems* are the policies that guide decision making. The synergistic energy created by integrating business and culture strategies drives the change process. Aligning systems and processes allows the change to run smoothly without stalling out or overheating. Figure 3 illustrates the integration of strategies supported by aligned systems and processes.

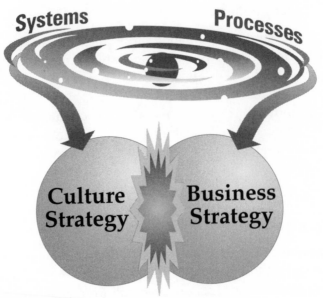

Figure 3. Aligning Processes and Systems with Culture and Business Strategies

Emphasis must be placed on aligning processes and systems to ensure that they encourage and reinforce the behaviors embedded in the culture strategy. An obvious example is an organization's compensation system. If leadership rewards sales associates for bringing in new customers rather than retaining old ones, then they clearly are valuing one behavior over the other. Sundstrand's experience provides a prime example of unaligned or misaligned processes and systems. Its failure to punish certain cultural behaviors gave its employees de facto encouragement to continue unethical behavior.

Changes at the systems and processes levels must be driven by senior leadership. The attention leaders give to alignment is critical because alignment ensures effective, long-term change. Without it the infrastructure of an organization will not be able to withstand the strain the change brings with it.

Measurement

In this book the term *measurement* will be revisited again and again. An organization must measure its long-term culture strategy just as it measures its business strategy. It must measure *what* goals will be reached and *how* they will be reached. Most organizations do measure their *lag indicators*—the *whats*, or outputs. Sales numbers, revenue, return on assets, economic value added, and other financial measures represent lag indicators.

However, reliance on lag measures can jeopardize an organization because it finds out too late in the process that its strategies weren't on target. Depending heavily on lag measures also ignores important, available up-front measurements. These are the *lead indicators*—the business strategies, or the *hows* of achieving the outputs measured by lag indicators. Few organizations measure lead indicators. For example, an organization can measure its strategy to move into an international market by contacting potential customers in a particular country or geographic region and surveying their interest in the products or services offered.

By analyzing the work of its research and development group in a given time frame, an organization can measure a strategy that calls for introducing three new products each year. Tracking the number of repeat customers allows the organization to measure not only a long-term customer retention strategy but also the profitability that results from customer retention. All these examples are lead indicators, but they also link lead indicators to lag indicators.

Historically, researchers have experienced difficulty in measuring aspects of culture, but this has changed in the past few years with Robert S. Kaplan and David P. Norton's development of the *balanced scorecard.* The balanced scorecard was designed for use in addition to standard measures of financial performance. It employs criteria that measure the health of businesses from three new perspectives: customers, internal business processes, and learning and growth. Kaplan and Norton see quantification in these areas as fitting hand in glove with financial measures.

Most recently, Kaplan and Norton have seen companies apply the scorecard to strategic management by linking short-term actions, which have been made measurable through the scorecard, with long-term strategies. Four key measures in the Kaplan-Norton method involve:

1. Building consensus around the vision and strategy through an integrated set of objectives and measures.

2. Management's communication of strategy throughout the organization, ensuring that departmental objectives are aligned with long-term strategy.

3. Business planning that allows integration of business and financial plans.

4. Performance feedback and learning that monitors short-term results.

These four key measures provide balance. However, adding one more step—placing greater emphasis on culture and cultural measurements in the balanced scorecard—will give leaders the ability to quantify aspects of culture and culture strategies during a change effort in the same way that they measure business strategies. This quantification is essential before and during organizational change to see that leaders have charted and maintained the proper course.

High-Involvement Change Strategy

In a change effort, involvement of the workforce is just as critical a component of the business and culture strategies as are alignment and measurement. It is essential for securing employee commitment and passion to help the effort succeed. The Meryl Reis Louis study in particular showed that having an organization's top echelon demonstrate beliefs does not guarantee that those beliefs will permeate the environment to generate an appropriate culture. People must have roles and responsibilities within the change effort so they will turn their energy toward organizational success.

Using high involvement in a change strategy appropriately involves people within the organization to develop and implement solutions that support the business and culture strategies. This builds upon the maxims that the people who perform a job know that job best and that involvement builds commitment. Breaking down this definition into its components will convey a clearer picture of the scope of such a change effort.

During this type of change, high involvement drives an organization toward its new direction through a systematic, rather than ad hoc, approach to involvement. The Sundstrand case illustrates such a systematic approach, with a highly visible CEO offering consistent communication, a restructuring of senior leadership to reflect the new culture, and a retraining effort that touched all employees.

Without a plan—one that takes into account the entire organization—good intentions disintegrate into unclear roles, avoidance of responsibility, and directionless activity. Senior leadership's rush to implement a culture change (perhaps a case of *wishing will make it so*) without appropriate involvement creates confusion. The authors recently worked with an organization that had just completed a four-hour session on high-performance work systems. At its conclusion the CEO stood up and said, "You are all empowered!" He might just as well have said, "Let the chaos begin!"

Saying that high involvement in a change strategy *appropriately involves people to develop and implement solutions* follows the reasoning that people inside the organization possess unique knowledge of its operation. However, the term *appropriate involvement* also implies a warning: Not all problems that accompany organizational change are solved by adding more people to the effort. Inappropriate involvement can bog down decision making. It's important to know when to involve a person or a group of people and when to trade long-term buy-in for short-term speed.

The Value-Driven Change Process

This book explores the design of a *value-driven change process* as a map for integrating business and culture strategies. The process is value driven because it strives to assure that the people implementing the change share, support, and practice a common set of beliefs or values. A fundamental tenet of organizational change is that workforce involvement is a tool for achieving change and future success. Figure 4 shows the four phases of the value-driven change process.

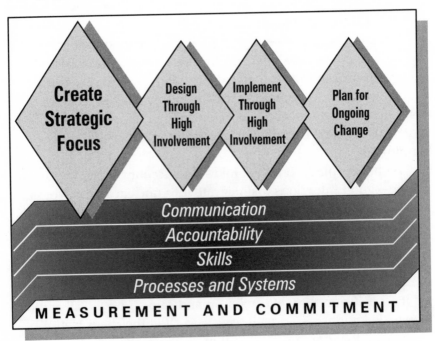

Figure 4. Value-Driven Change Model

The four phases of the process—from initial deliberations built around the question, *Where do you want to take your company?* through implementation and ongoing monitoring of the change effort—fully integrate the culture strategy with the business strategy, which is crucial for reasons already explained.

Measurement of both strategies is critical in all four phases of the process because what can't be measured can't be managed. All aspects of the business strategy and the culture strategy must be measurable in some way.

In phase one the organization creates a strategic focus with three key components:

1. **The vision**—The ideal future state the company wants to achieve in a three- to five-year time frame.

2. **Critical success factors**—Four or five key priorities, in terms of quantifiable outputs, that will allow the organization to leapfrog ahead in critical areas.

3. **Values**—Key behaviors that are instrumental in achieving and managing the future culture.

In phases two and three the organization puts together a structured approach to involve employees in leading and directing the change. If people are not involved in the design and implementation phases, they will resist the change. Only their involvement can build a culture that will drive business results. It will also secure the best ideas for change while assuring people's commitment and passion for the future state.

The framework for analyzing, designing, and adjusting the change effort rests in four areas, or organizational thrusts—communication, accountability, skills, and processes and systems. These thrusts become the focus for the many actions that drive change. Aligning these areas with the change effort removes barriers and assures that the processes and systems encourage and reinforce behaviors that demonstrate shared beliefs or values. It is an action-oriented approach that involves appropriate people within the organization.

In phase four, characterized by continuous monitoring and improvement, everyone involved in the change effort assesses progress and implements plans for ongoing improvement and change to realize the organization's vision.

The Importance of a Tailored Approach

Successful change implementation relies on a well-thought-out, tailored plan for many reasons, but primarily because each organization's *personality* creates a unique pattern of twists and turns that mark its road to change. For this reason the approach to change must be fitted to the organization's framework just as a suit of clothes is fitted to the body. This calls for redesigning particular systems and processes within the company to fit the business and culture strategies.

As mentioned earlier, the Buick Motor Division did just that. In response to foreign competition, executives at Buick, realizing the vital importance of creating a customer-focused environment, spearheaded a major culture change within the organization and at major-market auto dealerships.

Buick's new alignment, which included a stated vision of caring for customers as if they were family, inspired a shared set of values that helped modify behavior; establish customer-focused business objectives and measures; and align processes and systems with the stated vision, values, and objectives. This culture change emphasized and communicated Buick's ultimate priority to increase customer retention—a more profitable approach than constantly acquiring new business.

Development Dimensions International (DDI) has just entered the fifth year of its journey from a sales-driven company to one that focuses on the customer and customer retention. At the outset the operating committee used the value-driven change model to refine the corporate focus. Then the model guided leadership during significant realignments of processes and systems. Now it helps the company to stay on course and to channel organizational energy toward key business aspects that made, and continue to make, a real difference.

Because change becomes necessary in many organizations, as it became necessary at DDI, the goal of this book is to help others achieve effective organizational change by following a sound process, step-by-step, that will create a strategic focus, a committed workforce, and aligned systems and processes.

Creating a Strategic Focus

Many organizations' plans have little focus. It's not good enough to say, "We're headed here," or "We're trying to be this kind of company." Without focus strategic plans have many disparate elements and objectives, but no clear priorities and no consideration of the cultural side of the equation. The purpose of *strategic focus* is to identify *where* an organization is trying to go (through its vision), prioritize *what* it wants to achieve (through its critical success factors), and determine *how* it plans to reach its destination and achieve its goals (through its values). The focus is *strategic* because it addresses the long-term future of the company.

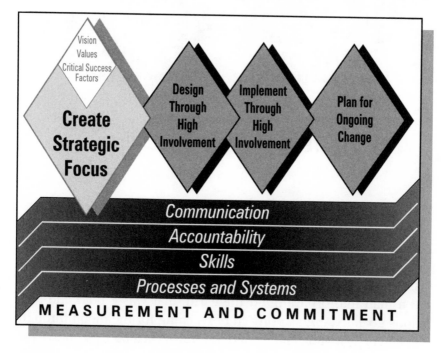

Figure 5. Value-Driven Change Model: Create Strategic Focus

A strategic focus grounds the business and culture strategies and allows them to be broken down into components. It directs an organization's energy to those key priorities that have formed its business strategies, thus facilitating a change effort and setting into motion the quest to achieve a new vision of success.

CHAPTER 3

STRATEGIC FOCUS AND THE VISION

In May 1961 President John F. Kennedy announced that the space program was moving from "low to high gear," and that America would land a man on the moon and return him safely to earth "before this decade is out." His statement reflected a vision to explore new frontiers. For a country that had never even put a man into orbit around the earth, that was a bold and ambitious goal. NASA's approach of reaching for the moon through the Mercury, Gemini, and Apollo programs became an initiative for achieving the vision to explore new frontiers.

Organizations do the same thing. They imagine what they want to achieve in the future and capture it in a statement that becomes a critical element of the strategic focus, and therefore of culture change. This is the *vision*—an ideal future state that an organization and its leaders would like to achieve. A vision explains to everyone inside and outside the organization where that entity is going.

An effective vision is concise and simple, and it illustrates an organization's uniqueness. It becomes a beacon of light that shows all stakeholders (employees, customers, suppliers, partners, and shareholders) where the organization is going and musters their commitment to reach the future state.

People often confuse corporate visions, which date back decades, with mission statements, objectives, and goals. A mission statement describes in great detail an organization's primary business and goals. It is often a dry definition of a business that looks at short-term goals; therefore, companies in similar markets tend to have similar mission statements. Wrangler, Levi Strauss, and Lee all have the mission to make jeans.

A written organizational vision, on the other hand, describes in a sentence or two the pinnacle an organization is striving to reach. A strong vision goes beyond a mission statement by providing a source of inspiration for everyone in the organization. It is their visions, not their missions, that convey how Wrangler, Levi Strauss, and Lee differ as organizations.

Creating a Sound Vision

Aside from being concise and unique to a particular company, a sound vision meets five important criteria. The organizational vision must:

- *State a nonfinancial goal with which most employees want to identify.* An organization's goals reflect its financial objectives. Its vision, however, includes goal-oriented, nonfinancial wording, such as best, world-class, preferred supplier, or leader.

- *Clearly define the organization's strategic advantage(s).* This element plays a large role in making a vision unique, and successful companies realize this fact. 3M considers innovation to be its strategic advantage, while L.L. Bean's is service, and Wal-Mart focuses on its distribution and inventory control. J.C. Penney looks at people—the consumers and the employees who serve them. Figure 6 shows the Penney Idea, which was written in 1913 and still is timely.

THE PENNEY IDEA

*To serve the public, as nearly as we can,
to its complete satisfaction.*

*To expect for the service we render a fair remuneration
and not all the profit the traffic will bear.*

*To do all in our power to pack the customer's dollar
full of value, quality, and satisfaction.*

*To continue to train ourselves and our associates
so that the service we give will be more and more
intelligently performed.*

To improve constantly the human factor in our business.

*To reward men and women in our organization through
participation in what the business produces.*

*To test our every policy, method, and act in this wise:
"Does it square with what is right and just?"*

Adopted 1913

Figure 6. Courtesy of the J.C. Penney Archives and Historical Museum

- *Have a realistic chance to succeed.* An organization develops an inspirational vision to help it strive and continue to progress, so the vision naturally will be a stretch. On the other hand, an unrealistic vision can cause frustration and become the subject of ridicule within the organization, particularly if people don't see any attempt to move toward it.

- *Inspire people.* Meeting this criterion usually depends on the spirit and often the wording of the vision. Unique, inspiring, even exciting language is appropriate and effective, providing it reflects a realistic vision.

- *Provide an "outsider-insider" perspective.* The vision should describe to an outsider what the organization will achieve and to an insider why he or she would want to work in that organization. The following example of a vision encompasses both perspectives: "To be the top manufacturer in the eyes of the customer (outsider's view) while providing an empowering place to work and maintaining an environment of trust and respect" (insider's view).

Consider these actual vision statements that generally meet most of the five criteria, while communicating the desired future state of the organization.

- **Industrial manufacturing organization:** To be the preferred supplier of fluid-carrying systems with an absolute commitment to our customers through empowered employees, advanced technology, and global capability.

- **Health care organization:** To be the region's preeminent, dominant leader in high-value, customer-oriented, compassionate, health-related services. To be recognized as a formidable, innovative, and stable entity and a vital, respected contributor to a healthy community. To be considered the best place to be employed because our work environment is fair, motivating, and challenging, respectful, honest, and caring; inspiring a feeling of teamwork, ownership, and partnership.

- **Local school district:** Our school district will be recognized as an exemplary school system with a reputation for setting standards of excellence. Together we will promote belonging and take pride in our ability to enable students to reach their fullest potential.
- **Manufacturing facility:** We will create an environment that will enable us to be the "plant of choice" in the development of new products that will support the needs of our global customers.

Measuring the Vision

Only a vision that can be measured has the potential to be realized. A claim to land a man on the moon can be wild talk or sincere belief, depending on the approach taken. An organization's leader merely engages in rhetoric by saying, "We are going to be the best," "the preferred supplier," or "one of the leading organizations." A vision with no clear way to determine progress can be perceived by an already cynical workforce as leadership's latest publicity stunt—that the people at the top lack the commitment to achieve real change.

A large pharmaceutical company included *world-class* as part of its ideal future state. But after a year's time, the CEO failed to see evidence that the vision of world-class had changed behavior or motivated people to accept the vision. He knew something was missing and took action.

To address the problem, leaders were asked to cite specific parameters for world-class—what it meant to the organization in concrete business terms. The CEO admitted that no one ever defined measures for marking progress toward the achievement of that goal. In subsequent meetings the CEO and senior executives then defined world-class for their industry in terms of being "the supplier of choice for cardiovascular pulmonary drugs in the eyes of their customers." This vision was measurable because the industry collected customer-preference information on an annual basis. From that point on, each time someone mentioned world-class, they also mentioned the customer-preference information.

Many organizations include *to be the best* in their visions. One such company, a maker of dry shaving products, realized a market share of only 13 percent, which was dwarfed by the biggest competitor's 61 percent market share. Obviously, for the smaller company being *the best* could not translate into market share and/or revenue. Instead, the company defined *the best* with two quality measures rated as important by customers in industrywide market surveys—*closeness of the shave* and *safety*. Using these measures, the company arrived at a clear, realistic vision in relation to its competitors.

All this drives home the point that for a vision to direct people and rally them toward a common purpose, progress must be shown in some way—the vision must be measurable. Dr. W. Edwards Deming, one of the fathers of quality improvement, indicated in many of his works that the first point of a quality movement is the creation of a constancy of purpose—a commitment to stay the course. An appropriate, well-articulated, measurable vision becomes the vehicle that will maintain this constancy throughout a change effort.

Shared Understanding

Occasionally, the concept of vision becomes the object of scorn and ridicule in the shark-infested waters of the organizational world. In a 1996 *Fortune* magazine article, Thomas A. Stewart says, "Visions are Big, Important Stuff everyone's supposed to subscribe to. The easiest way to do that is to drain them of substance so nothing remains to disagree with. Most visions boil down to 'Go, team, go!'" (p. 195). Stewart alludes to the fact that a vision can become political, with each department in an organization pushing for its own best interest.

This type of "virtual vision" winks at the concept just to satisfy internal or external pressure. But nothing could be worse for an organization than to develop a flawed or disingenuous vision. With such a leaky hull, the change effort is bound to sink, leaving survivors to fend for themselves in treacherous waters.

In his book *The Fifth Discipline*, author Peter M. Senge (1990) identifies the need within organizations to foster commitment to vision, not merely compliance or *going along with the program.* He states that it sometimes becomes difficult to sort out who is committed to the vision and who merely complies with it, but that there is a great difference between them.

> The committed person brings an energy, passion, and excitement that cannot be generated if you are only compliant, even genuinely compliant. The committed person doesn't play by the "rules of the game." He is responsible for the game. If the rules of the game stand in the way of achieving the vision, he will find ways to change the rules. A group of people truly committed to a common vision is an awesome force. They can accomplish the seemingly impossible (p. 221).

Even the best-intentioned leaders often don't take the steps necessary to secure this kind of commitment. They put great time and effort into creating their vision for the company—and almost none into making sure people understand and follow it. They post it in the lobby and publish it in the annual report, and customers see it on the letterhead. Consider the wasted time and effort—and the missed opportunity to realize a shared understanding and, more importantly, a shared commitment.

Leaders at the Buick Motor Division created a vision, *Customer Care That Says You're Family.* To back it up, they developed a two-fold approach. They facilitated a culture change in support of the vision throughout 500 dealerships. Then they ensured that their employees possessed the hands-on skills they needed not only to meet but to exceed customer expectations—both internally and externally. Their success depended on having customers who were both satisfied and enthusiastic.

As Buick proves, what you put into a vision equals what the vision is capable of achieving. If used wisely, with knowledge and sincerity, an organizational vision becomes a powerful source of direction, inspiration, and motivation. Without the proper thought, it can carelessly aim people toward a short-lived, narrow task at hand. A familiar old story illustrates this difference:

A passerby asked four workers at a construction site what they were doing. The first worker described the task: "I'm laying brick." The second described the goal: "I'm building walls." The third gave the mission: "I'm building a cathedral." The fourth described his role as, "I'm creating a place where people will come to explore the joy and sorrow of life, give thanks, and ask for guidance. When they leave, they will help create a better world." That fourth worker captured in two sentences the essence and spirit of a vision.

All these workers described some aspect of their work, each with a broader view of its purpose and power than the one before. This comprehensive view—the ability to see the "big picture"—is the key to creating a culture that uses high-performance work systems to achieve organizational change. Understanding the vision and all its implications draws upon the energy of everyone in the organization and, at the same time, provides a personal source of empowerment that drives initiative and improvement. The vision becomes the force that calls all hands on deck to man a successful change voyage.

CHAPTER 4

STRATEGIC FOCUS AND
CRITICAL SUCCESS FACTORS

The vision is the call—the inspiration to persevere, to continue on in the voyage of change. But, vision not withstanding, voyages don't just happen. They take meticulous planning. Between President Kennedy's announced intention to land a man on the moon and actual touchdown on the lunar surface fell an eight-year span of details for NASA that encompassed *how* to do it. Launching a rocket from the spinning earth to a moon moving at 2,200 miles per hour—more than 200,000 miles away. Developing computer technology far in advance of anything that had come before. Providing an environment in which men could survive on a voyage from one place to the other, and back again. Sending one vehicle, the lunar module, to the surface of the moon while the command module orbited. Launching the lunar module from the moon and docking with the command module—more moving targets. Funding it all in a decade of turbulence. How NASA met these challenges would mean success or failure of the vision.

Any organizational change brings with it such issues. The sheer drama of men sitting atop a flaming rocket becomes the drama of success or failure of the organization, its profitability, the job security of men and women, and the quality of life of their children. The critical *whats* translate from physics, rocket propulsion, computer technology, environmental controls, and spaceflight personnel to such areas as markets, products and services, customers, sales/delivery distribution, and people. These form key long-term business strategies that the leadership believes will help achieve the vision.

As leaders articulate and refine these key strategies, they also begin to consider improvements for strengthening the organization's competitive position in each strategic category. Following are categories of business strategies important to most organizations.

Markets

A market is a geographical location, a demographic group of consumers, or a type of industry. Companies target their products and services to specific markets. A key market strategy might involve expanding into major international markets to become a global player, reaching certain niche markets, or serving consumers in a particular demographic group.

Products and Services

A products and services strategy addresses long-term actions that will ensure prospects or clients perceive a company's offerings as preferable to the competition's. This strategy might include moving from traditional areas of operations into new ones, phasing out products, and introducing new products. A good example would be the "big six" accounting firms expanding from audit/tax services into consulting services. One company's products strategy might be one-stop shopping with an array of products and services while another's is to be the best in a specific area.

Products and services strategies can also involve introducing new products within a given time frame (companies like Rubbermaid) or heavy research and development (pharmaceutical companies). Improving development of products or services in terms of quality, cycle time, and design will move any organization closer to its vision.

Customers

The type of customer relationships an organization seeks determines this strategy. One company might concentrate on building
long-term partnerships with customers, stressing retention and
loyalty, which affects all customer-relation functions on a daily
basis. Another company might have a "transaction" strategy that
focuses on the sale of a commodity on a one-time basis, with no
goal for long-term relationships.

Sales/Delivery Distribution

This category relates to the way a product or service reaches
customers. An organization might use a dedicated sales force as its
distribution channel or use brokers or third parties, as does the
insurance industry. Other organizations might use catalogs, the
Internet, televised commercials, or home-shopping networks to
reach their markets. In reality most organizations' sales/delivery
distribution strategies include a combination of methods. The
main issue is to make sure the strategy is appropriate for the
organization's direction.

People

This strategy relates to the degree to which an organization
values its people and how it involves them in achieving objectives.
For example, for some organizations, attracting, developing, and
retaining high-quality employees might be a critical strategy in
achieving the vision. Other organizations might perceive prosperity as the result of hiring outside talent at high levels. Where
some businesses clearly see people as an investment, others might
view them as an expense. Some organizations expect high levels of
involvement and therefore provide extensive skills training; yet,
for other companies, involvement isn't even a factor. These per-
ceptions of the impact and value of people directly correlate to the
way in which they are treated.

Critical Success Factors Defined

Once an organization has developed a business strategy that
addresses these five categories, it must translate that strategy into
specific, long-term goals. *Critical success factors* (CSFs) are subsets of

the strategies and provide the four or five highest impact opportunities to propel an organization ahead of its competition. They are catalysts for focusing energy and achieving business strategies.

Critical success factors define issues that are barriers to the success of an organization and its vision. Limiting the number to four or five issues ensures that attention is focused solidly in their direction. CSFs make it easier to answer the question, "What needs to be done to achieve the organization's vision?" They direct human energy toward specific, market-driven, operational areas that will achieve the company's vision if addressed, or jeopardize the future of the company if ignored.

In terms of Kennedy's 1961 vision of exploring new frontiers, critical success factors might have included, "Develop computer technology to support the project" and "Secure adequate funding for the program." Such CSFs would have dealt with a few of the major challenges facing NASA in the 60s.

The following examples of critical success factors include some that are external (related to expanding in a market or retaining customers) and internal (related to developing new technology or reducing cycle time).

- Attract, develop, and retain knowledgeable, high-caliber associates.
- Develop manufacturing innovations to eliminate waste, improve productivity, and add value for our customers.
- Ensure professional, nonconfrontational sales and service processes and interactions.
- Establish strategic alliances with suppliers to improve our product and process quality.
- Increase customer retention rate.
- Reduce the cycle time of getting products to market.
- Improve the quality and accessibility of client and operational information.
- Achieve universal compliance with laws and regulations 100 percent of the time.
- Build community trust and respect.

- Continuously improve product quality.

- Develop compatible processes and systems worldwide.

Well-articulated, prominently displayed CSFs help people understand a change effort as concrete actions within the context of their day-to-day work and activities. CSFs also prompt leaders to stay focused on critical issues. Experience with hundreds of organizations reveals that senior leaders don't do this easily; they tend to deal with too many issues. This is the Achilles' heel of the senior leadership function. It leads to fuzzy focus and unclear priorities. Well-thought-out, clear CSFs, however, take the guesswork out of prioritizing. They clearly communicate to everyone the four or five most crucial elements an organization needs to attend to in order to maintain and enhance its competitive position. Figure 7 lists indicators of common organizational problems and the type of CSFs that will address them.

Problem Indicators	CSFs to Address
■ Loss of 20 percent of customers each year. ■ Sales emphasis on new customers only. ■ Decreased profit. ■ Decreased market share.	**Customer Retention**
■ Long lead times. ■ Opportunities lost because of late entry into the market. ■ Deadlines missed.	**Cycle Time Reduction**
■ High turnover. ■ Competitors taking key employees. ■ Rising training and recruiting costs.	**Employee Retention**
■ Loss of market share. ■ Shrinking markets. ■ New competitors.	**New Products and Services**

Figure 7. Common Organizational Problems and Related CSFs

Identifying and Designing Critical Success Factors

Even though they might be broad in scope, well-designed critical success factors must be measured. They must also be specific enough to channel and sustain organizational energy for more than a year; the common rate is three to five years. This is critical because most organizations' CSFs cannot be accomplished within a short time frame. For example, the CSF *Expansion in the European market* might take years to accomplish. Initiatives or short-term actions, such as *Acquire ISO9000 certification* or *Hire employees with foreign language skills,* will help achieve this particular critical success factor, but they are focused too narrowly to serve as CSFs themselves.

The following questions can help determine the effectiveness of critical success factors.

- *Do our CSFs represent the four or five most critical areas within the organization that need major improvement?* As stated before, focusing energy on major improvement efforts in these critical areas for the next three to five years can vault an organization ahead of the competition. That's exactly what happened with a company whose vision was to *become a global organization.* This organization initially encountered a barrier in attempting to make operations consistent with the image it presented to large, multinational customers. Senior leaders soon learned that realizing their vision required developing processes and systems that would be compatible worldwide.

  The company then made *Compatibility of processes and systems* one of its critical success factors. It took more than three years to achieve this CSF, but overcoming this barrier gave the company a huge advantage over competitors still struggling with the consistency issue.

- *Do our CSFs drive key business initiatives and strategies that will expand business or increase market share?* An organization usually targets as its CSFs those issues that are perceived as barriers to its success. For example, some businesses might target increased market share as a CSF. In reality, increased market share is the *output* of doing something different. CSFs are areas that, if addressed, would best help the business increase its market share. Therefore, increased market share is *not* the CSF, it is the result (or output) of doing something different to achieve that desired goal. Too often, organizations that don't achieve their business goals focus on an output without focusing on what it takes to achieve it. That's why these success factors are called *critical*.

To establish a CSF, a company should ask, "What is it in our business that's preventing us from improving our market share?" Perhaps it's customer retention. Perhaps it's employee turnover. If so, these areas would then become CSFs. A CSF is what must be done to achieve increased market share, such as *Improve customer satisfaction* or *Reduce employee turnover* or whatever the organization determines has hindered it from increasing market share.

It's important to remember that critical success factors are not financial targets. Financial targets, like profitability, revenue, and market share, tend to be *measures* of CSFs. Too often, companies scrutinize the output they want to realize rather than the key actions that will produce the output. Financial results are the output of doing the right things—the kinds of things embodied in the CSFs. However, financial indicators can and do serve as appropriate measures of progress in achieving critical success factors.

- **Do our CSFs specifically state action-oriented targets?** As mentioned before, CSFs must be specific enough to command and maintain people's attention and energy on concrete action. Statements such as *Improve customer service* or *Reduce cycle time* head in the right direction, but would achieve stronger results if their language were more specific. *Improve customer service* would then become *Increase responsiveness to customers by giving more authority to frontline employees*. *Reduce cycle time* would read *Reduce cycle time in getting products to market*.

- *Are our CSFs measurable?* Because CSFs constitute the *what needs to be done* part of the vision, it's imperative that they can be measured. In actuality, desired outputs stated within a time frame usually form the measure. A critical success factor for ITT A-C Pump (a unit of ITT Industries), a Cincinnati, Ohio, industrial pump manufacturer, is *Strengthen market channels in selected geographical areas.* Measures for that CSF are sales by market territory, number of new distributors, and expanded capacity within distributors. Other examples of typical CSF measures are increased volume, market share, and customer satisfaction levels, all of which would be measured within a defined time frame.

As stated earlier, financial measures do not meet the criteria to serve as critical success factors. However, such measures as revenue or profits, and ratios like ROI, ROE, or ROA might be ways to gauge progress in achieving a CSF. Some organizations consider poor results in one or more of these areas as symptoms that leaders are not giving enough attention to CSFs and the culture that supports them.

Gathering Data to Determine Critical Success Factors

To develop CSFs that will achieve an organization's unique vision, leaders use environmental scans to gather information and analyze both the internal and external environments in which the company operates. The scans involve formal surveys or informal conversations with employees and customers as well as competitive and industry studies.

An *external* environmental information scan identifies the requirements and expectations that are most important to the customer. An *internal* scan identifies organizational drivers as well as barriers to meeting requirements and expectations.

Combined external and internal scans provide optimal interpretation of what is happening within the culture of an organization. This continual process of external and internal scanning produces data that can be compiled and revisited frequently to check progress in terms of culture change.

Conducted formally or informally, these scans can also trigger ongoing awareness and analysis. Formal feedback provides quantitative data that directs leaders' attention to what the majority of customers want. Informal feedback provides rich qualitative data used in building the kind of unique relationship that leads to customer satisfaction. The cycle illustrated in Figure 8 generates critical success factors that continually review and refine a change effort, which is in itself an ongoing process.

	External Scan	**Internal Scan**
Formal	▪ Customer surveys ▪ Market research ▪ Customer project reviews ▪ Customer complaints ▪ Lost sales analysis ▪ Service audits	▪ Employee surveys ▪ Culture/Climate audits ▪ Quality audits ▪ Exit interviews ▪ Associate/Department feedback forms ▪ Focus group meetings
Informal	▪ Client contacts ▪ Discussions with suppliers, competitors ▪ Client feedback from field associates ▪ Anecdotal competitor information	▪ Conversations ▪ Impromptu meetings and discussions with leaders, field, sales force, service technicians, and other employees

Figure 8. CSFs Information Scan Cycle

CSF Measurement

Specific CSFs, such as *Reduce cycle time, Increase customer loyalty,* or *Retain high-caliber employees,* are clearly measurable. CSFs such as *Increase responsiveness to customers, Implement compatible processes worldwide,* or *Utilize nonconfrontational sales and service processes* aren't measured as easily. However, they typify CSFs that are crucial for many organizations, and the effort to measure them will pay off in concrete action that drives progress. If an organization finds itself struggling to identify specific measurements for a particular CSF, then the specificity of that CSF needs to be reconsidered.

Considering a few scenarios might help explain the process of measuring critical success factors. If an organization's senior leaders were measuring a CSF related to improving customer loyalty, they would look at customer retention rates. They would also look at figures concerning the customers' likelihood to repurchase, to recommend that others purchase from the company, or to name the company as a preferred supplier or partner.

Many organizations recognize *Attracting, developing, and retaining high-caliber associates* as an appropriate CSF, but again, measurement could be complicated. The retaining component is simple—track employee turnover. The attracting, developing part is not as easy to measure. Attracting might be measured by the cycle time in recruiting—that is, average length of time from open position to hire. Creating a measure for developing is even tougher. Some organizations track the measure "promotions into key positions from within versus hiring from the outside." Training and skills acquired per employee per year or the number of backup candidates in place also might be effective development measures.

Analysis, scanning, focusing, strategizing—the map for change is finally taking shape. The destination (vision), *where* the organization wants to go, is charted. *What* needs to be done specifically to reach the destination via the critical success factors has been determined. The next step is to define the culture that supports the vision and the CSFs—a step that involves organizational *values*.

CHAPTER 5

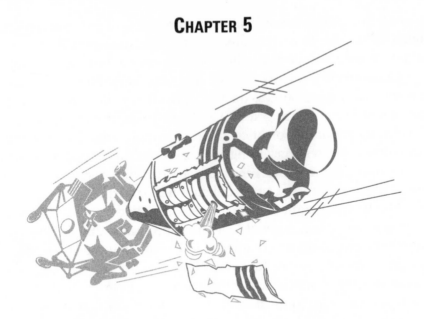

STRATEGIC FOCUS AND THE VALUES

☆ ☆ ☆

The concept of organizational values can perhaps best be illustrated not by Apollo 11, with its flawless execution of a trip to the moon, but by Apollo 13. This mission became a study in human survival when a liquid oxygen tank exploded aboard its service module 31 hours after liftoff. In a matter of seconds, the journey's goal shifted from landing astronauts on the moon for a third time to keeping three human beings alive 200,000 miles from earth—in a damaged spacecraft with inadequate power and oxygen to make it back home.

The command at Kennedy Space Center and at Mission Control in Houston became a model of teamwork, with a commitment to one thought: These three men—friends and colleagues—must not die. Three hundred controllers and technicians worked around the clock—checking their calculations again and again, jury-rigging equipment, running simulations, making decisions with both speed and care—and ultimately achieved their goal. Apollo 13 splashed down in the Atlantic three and a half days after the explosion.

Armed with collaboration, dedication, know-how, and care for human life, the men and women in Florida and Texas helped the three astronauts survive and demonstrated a set of beliefs that reflected Peter Senge's statement mentioned earlier: "A group of people truly committed to a common vision is an awesome force. They can accomplish the seemingly impossible."

Crises often reveal the true culture of an organization. This type of volatile situation rocked Johnson & Johnson from September 29 to October 1, 1982. During those three days, Tylenol® contaminated with cyanide (the perpetrator was later tried and convicted) was ingested by consumers, causing seven deaths. Immediately, Johnson & Johnson pulled all product from the shelves and developed tamper-proof packaging. Despite the resulting economic loss, the company's commitment to public safety was firm and led to a strong economic rebound in a short time.

When a little girl named Jessica fell down a well in Texas on October 14, 1987, a Federal Express employee authorized the $30,000 expense to ship by air a special drill that ultimately helped rescue Jessica two days later. This decision, made without the approval of higher-ups, agreed with a strong customer service focus within Federal Express.

The leadership at both Johnson & Johnson and Federal Express fostered a strongly positive culture, which ultimately led to achieving the business strategy and, more importantly, causing employees to do the right thing and save lives. This high standard of doing the right thing can drive an organization toward success. It can also strike a responsive chord with customers.

On the other hand, failure to manage organizational culture and adhere to a set of commonly shared beliefs can create a negative culture, as at the Sundstrand Corporation, with its old environment of *anything goes* in the name of profit. Negative cultures can cause tremendous public relations problems and affect organizational success, particularly when customers begin to question unethical behavior. For one oil company, a negative culture meant that a ship's captain consumed alcohol on the job, resulting in a massive oil spill and subsequent scandal. For another oil company it meant that minorities were not hired or promoted, leading to charges of racial discrimination.

Values Defined

Hopefully, at this point the importance of developing and combining business and culture strategies and of managing organizational culture to achieve those strategies is evident. The question now is, "How does an organization get its people to implement the strategies and live the culture?" The answer is by establishing a fundamental set of beliefs or principles that delineate and endorse supportive behaviors. These beliefs, or principles, are an organization's values.

Values are subtle mechanisms that informally convey the behaviors that are sanctioned and prohibited within the organization. They let people know—across all business functions—how to achieve the vision. Values determine behaviors, which, in turn, reinforce the values. Whether they are labeled as "common shared values" or "guiding principles," values create the culture that supports achieving the vision and the critical success factors. Figure 9 illustrates the values, culture, and behavior relationship.

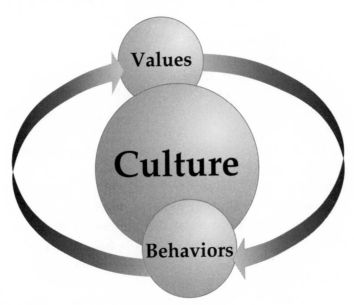

Figure 9. Values drive behavior; behavior reinforces values.

Managing and Supporting the Values

Published success stories of companies such as Scandinavian Air Systems, Saturn, Wal-Mart, Federal Express, and General Electric (GE) underscore the importance of a supportive set of values. In fact, under Jack Welch's leadership, GE exemplifies the strongest type of support for people who live the values. In GE's 1991 annual report as well as many other writings, Welch outlined his support for GE's values of *speed, boundlessness,* and *involvement* by defining the types of leaders he wants at GE. He describes four types of leaders and their probable destinies:

Type of Leader	Probable Destiny
1. Leaders who hit their numbers and live the GE values	Promotion
2. Leaders who don't hit their numbers but live the values	Second chance
3. Leaders who hit their numbers but don't live the values	Dismissal
4. Leaders who don't hit their numbers or live the values	Dismissal

It's understandable why category 4 leaders are dismissed. But Welch believes that even though they hit their numbers, leaders in category 3 should also leave the company because they fail to live the values and therefore negatively affect both those around them and the long-term success of the company.

Saturn is another company that lives the values. Saturn's parent, General Motors, saw the need for a culture change that would reverse Saturn's assembly-line attitude, which favored robots and devalued people. Saturn's culture and advertising now reflect the value of quality and prominently feature the people who produce that quality.

Authors Benjamin Schneider, Arthur P. Brief, and Richard A. Guzzo point to IBM, Hewlett-Packard, and the J.C. Penney Company, among others, as organizations whose cultures reflect the values of their founders. In a 1996 *Organizational Dynamics* article, they break such legacies down into style, practices, and procedures—in effect, "the founder's imprint." They then point out that within organizations where such a legacy is strong, present-day employees can lose sight of the founder's vision and values but still be bound to what they don't really understand. In the end this can lead to people answering queries about processes with a shrug and a, "We've always done things that way. I don't know why."

This example illustrates the belief that organizations must actively manage the culture and live the values and that this process is perpetual. In effect, every decision and every action of everyone from the CEO down must support and model the behaviors that senior leadership identifies as crucial to the organization's success.

Organizations that do not have a set of values, or that do not support the values they *do* have, usually achieve an environment tainted by cynicism and distrust. In this type of company, people worry about internal, political, or turf issues instead of zeroing in on customers and competitors.

On the other hand, organizations that strongly support and manage their values dramatically improve their chances of success. This is true across the organizational spectrum, regardless of a company's size or type. At one extreme is a public institution like the Chartiers Valley School District near Pittsburgh. The district recognized the necessity of focusing on service to the community and developed a set of values that centered on shared, community, parent-student involvement; delivery of quality education; and selection and development of teachers who would live the values.

This commitment to a solid strategic focus led to the district being named by *Money Magazine* in 1996 as one of the top 100 school districts in its class in the U.S. The districts were judged in five categories, including enthusiastic teachers, innovative administrators, and high expectations for all students.

At the opposite end of the organizational spectrum, large companies, such as Tennessee Eastman and Texas Instruments, have won the Malcolm Baldrige Award for quality, due in part to a push within each organization for increased teamwork and personal involvement.

These organizations, and many others like them, present overwhelming evidence of what can be accomplished by visible commitment to the creation and management of a set of shared values. This type of commitment propels organizations past the buy-in stage and well into the challenging universe of realizing their culture-change goals.

Identifying Organizational Values

Perhaps the easiest way for senior leaders to start thinking about values is to ask five basic questions. When examining their vision of the future state of the organization, leaders can quiz themselves with:

1. *What do we want our customers/suppliers to say about our organization when we're not in the room?* Any organization with a vision of success probably wants to be perceived as listening to customer needs and being responsive, proactive, and flexible. The goal of such an organization will be to foster relationships that feel like partnerships. It will want to avoid a perception of rigidity and bureaucracy.

2. *How do we want our employees to answer the question, "What's it like to work around here?"* Employees of most successful organizations want leaders to listen to their ideas. They want to feel respected and valued. They seek some degree of control over their jobs.

3. *What are our organization's priorities in terms of which behaviors are rewarded and which are punished?* The rank and file should be able to discuss problems and deliver bad news without fear of the messenger being shot. Likewise, they should be encouraged to take appropriate risks. On the other hand, behaviors such as avoiding action, ignoring the customer, and failing to work with internal departments and colleagues must be deemed unacceptable.

4. *As leaders, what can we do that will demonstrate the future state?* If the desired future state includes a strong customer service focus, leaders should be spending time with customers, asking for their input in decision making, and making customer satisfaction a top priority.

5. *If we were hiring all new employees, what characteristics would we be looking for?* A highly responsive organization comprises individuals with common traits, such as the initiative to meet customer needs, a willingness to be a team player, a disposition toward action, and the ability to learn.

Serious thinking about these five questions can help identify a tentative list of values that best demonstrate the desired culture. At this point, a process that includes surveys, focus groups, and consensus discussions within the organization will shape a final list of four to six organizational values. Four to six values work well for nearly all organizations. Fewer leave too much cultural ambiguity; more can become unwieldy.

To further target employee energy in a change effort, most organizations identify one *driving value*. The driving value, of paramount importance, takes precedence over the others. A driving value helps people set priorities and make decisions, particularly when two or more organizational values seem to be conflicting. For example, the value of *Superior Customer Service* sometimes conflicts with values such as *Quality of Life* or *Teamwork*. Such a conflict raises difficult questions. Should an associate sacrifice a Saturday to get a product out the door on time? Or should the Saturday be considered sacrosanct and the customer deadline extended?

Conflicts between customer service and quality create even more difficult situations because of the basic struggle to make delivery dates while assuring product quality. Satisfying the need for one can sometimes mean sacrificing another. In situations like these, a driving value can end the struggle and break the tie.

With the driving value in place, the other three to five values become *supporting* or *facilitating* values that complement the primary value. Defined in this way, the entire roster of values clashes less frequently, and employees gain a clearer understanding of the character of the place in which they work. In effect, values help align the personalities of all employees with the personality of the organization.

Figure 10 builds upon Figure 7 to show common cultural deficiencies that exist within organizations, and it links these with values that can address those deficiencies.

Problem Indicators	CSFs to Address	Cultural Deficiencies	Values to Address
■ Loss of 20 percent of customers each year. ■ Sales emphasis on new customers only. ■ Decreased profit. ■ Decreased market share.	Customer Retention	■ Customer service not important. ■ Lack of innovation in meeting customer needs. ■ No teamwork between field and headquarters operations.	Customer Service
■ Long lead times. ■ Opportunities lost because of late entry into the market. ■ Deadlines missed.	Cycle Time Reduction	■ Decisions bogged down in multiple approvals. ■ Employees don't have ability or responsibility to make decisions.	Empowerment
■ High turnover. ■ Competitors taking key employees. ■ Rising training and recruiting costs.	Employee Retention	■ Employees not challenged. ■ Employees treated like "pairs of hands." ■ Employees not trusted to make decisions.	Empowerment
■ Loss of market share. ■ Shrinking markets. ■ New competitors.	New Products and Services	■ No innovation. ■ Creativity, innovation, and suggestions not encouraged. ■ Ideas criticized quickly and not given a chance.	Innovation

Figure 10. Linking Values with Common Organizational Cultural Deficiencies

Living the Values

At this point in the process of organizational change, many organizations fall into a trap. They work through lengthy meetings to identify a list of values, which then remain words on paper— great potential relegated to wall signs that become part of the scenery, eventually unseen and forgotten. Identifying a list of values and committing them to paper is an important step, but it's only a step. The values must be meaningful to each employee in terms of behaviors and motivations. They become meaningful only if supported by a description that makes their purpose clear. Without such a description, the values remain merely words, and in fact, risk becoming a target of cynicism.

A value description is a clear definition of the value in the form of a statement that explains its importance to the company, including concrete examples or best practices that illustrate the value in action. Figure 11 shows a complete value description from Blue Cross and Blue Shield of Montana.

Quality

Description
Blue Cross and Blue Shield of Montana seeks to maintain or exceed service quality and reliability for our customers.

Importance
A high-level, quality product will allow us to maintain and improve our competitive advantage. Encouraging all employees to seek top-quality outcomes in all of their endeavors will ensure the highest quality.

Best Practices
- We will publish corporate and departmental goals for all employees.
- We will communicate team and individual goals to teams and individuals.
- We will give feedback on progress toward goals.
- We will provide team and job training to all individuals.
- We will provide cross-training for team members.
- We will constantly examine processes for opportunities to simplify and remove non-value-added tasks.

Figure 11. Blue Cross and Blue Shield of Montana's Quality Value: A Complete Description

Organizational values are powerful tools for redefining culture, but as such, they can do as much harm as good because *not* living them creates cynicism and mistrust. It all depends on how they're used. Stated simply, leaders can't just talk about values. They have to demonstrate them with everything they say and do, every decision they make, and every interaction they have with an employee—from the boardroom to the mail room. If leadership fails to do this, it faces the prospect of dealing with a different, opposing set of values than originally planned.

How many times have senior leaders said that they want open and constant communication in order to stay in touch with the daily operations of the organization? These same leaders then shoot so many messengers that people see the bodies lying around and refuse to pass on bad news. When this happens, open communication becomes a myth or a company joke instead of reality. Too often organizations preach teamwork and collaboration while permitting day-to-day behaviors that create everything from petty scuffles over turf to blatant interdepartmental rivalry.

T.J. and Sandar Larkin feel strongly that communicating the values by merely talking about them is ineffective. In their 1996 *Harvard Business Review* article they say, "The only effective way to communicate a value is to act in accordance with it and give others the incentive to do the same" (p. 96).

They further point to the cynicism of the workplace and hint at the potentially negative side of creating a set of values. "If you break the rule that values are best communicated through actions, employees will punish you" (p. 96). Typically, this punishment takes the form of passive-aggressive behavior from employees who don't understand leadership's behaviors and therefore can't support them. Creating a set of values raises expectations for change and improvement. Failure to live those values can lead to more damage than the lack of values caused in the first place.

Rebuilding lost trust and creating a culture in which people can commit their energy and enthusiasm require that leaders continually model, communicate, and support shared values. Senior leaders can't advertise their way into a culture change. They must live and reinforce the values. As tempting as it might be to publish and post the values and declare the process completed, they must resist the temptation. Instead, they need to be out there leading by example, demonstrating the values until those values become reality for everyone in the organization.

If an organization champions customer service, then it must support customer-oriented decisions, as did Federal Express when one of its employees authorized the $30,000 expense to ship a drill to Texas. If ethical conduct is deemed a primary value, then an organization will encourage whistle-blowing and follow through with ethics training, as did the Sundstrand Corporation.

Many more examples of values in action are within easy reach. L.L. Bean is known for its customer service and quality. Recently a customer service team (CST) representative was placing a phone order for a customer and discovered that the item, an Ellie Bear wearing a sweatshirt, was on back order. (Actually, the bear was available, but its sweatshirt was not.) The rep apologized to the disappointed customer and found out that the bear had been ordered for a child suffering with leukemia in Boston Children's Hospital. The CST rep himself had ordered a bear for delivery at Christmas and suggested that the customer purchase the unclothed bear, and he would send the sweatshirt from his own bear directly to the child in the hospital.

Unfortunately, the rep's bear came unclothed as well (sweatshirts were still on back order). The rep posted a sign in a common area requesting an Ellie Bear sweatshirt. Soon after, two other employees located a sweatshirt and mailed it to the child in the hospital. The CST leader submitted the rep's story to the in-house newsletter, believing that people who care about the customer need to be recognized because they "have made L.L. Bean the company it is today."

People will live the values only if leaders live them as well. There is no substitute for demonstrations of organizational values by a president, CEO, or vice president. Speeches aren't enough. Booklets aren't enough. They're important because they convey the concepts—but they're not enough. It remains a leadership responsibility to live the values and set the example that others will follow.

Measuring the Effectiveness of Values

Measurement provides concrete information about how well leaders and employees live the values. An effective way to gather this data is an internal survey containing questions that ask how well people are demonstrating the best practices. Survey feedback then provides the basis for actions that will improve the strength of the values. Senior leaders who are serious about values and culture measure how well the values are being demonstrated. However, they also measure how well leaders are living them. Figure 12 lists the wide variety of core values many organizations use. Figure 13 lists three values and associated sample survey questions designed to gauge the effectiveness of those values within the organization.

Product/Service Delivery Values	▪ Customer Service ▪ Constant Improvement ▪ Innovation ▪ Quality
Time/Change Orientation Values	▪ Bias for Action ▪ Organizational Flexibility ▪ Long-Term Focus
Interpersonal Relationships Values	▪ Empowerment ▪ Teamwork ▪ Open Communication ▪ Integrity
Employee Treatment Values	▪ Concern for People ▪ Development of People ▪ Quality of Life for Associates ▪ Valuing Diversity
Environment/ Resources Values	▪ Community Responsibility ▪ Resource Consciousness ▪ Safety

Figure 12. Core Values

CUSTOMER SERVICE

People I work with:

X | Resolve customer problems on the spot whenever possible.

Leaders of my work group:

X | Share customer service results with employees.

X | Pay close attention to customer service when evaluating employees' performance.

EMPOWERMENT

People I work with:

X | Participate in making decisions that affect the work group.

X | Have easy access to all the resources they need to do a good job.

Leaders of my work group:

X | Coach employees on challenging assignments without taking over.

X | Delegate tasks that increase employees' level of responsibility and involvement.

TEAMWORK

People I work with:

X | Willingly help others no matter where such people work in the organization.

X | Have specific team goals that everyone supports.

Leaders of my work group:

X | Reward employees for team efforts.

X | Create alliances with other teams and departments.

X | Promote mutual problem solving with internal customers and suppliers.

Figure 13. Survey Questions for Customer Service, Empowerment, and Teamwork Values

In addition to survey data that provide the primary, statistical source of information about living the values, a variety of sources can provide additional data. Leaders can simply observe others' behavior. They might also convene focus groups or town meetings or set up executive lunches to gather informal feedback. In their decision-making meetings leaders can assess how each decision supports, or fails to support, the organization's values.

All these methods provide information that highlights areas in which practices still need to be aligned with the values. In reality, reviewing behaviors to make sure they reflect the values is an ongoing process. If the commitment to live a set of values is real, everyone—every day—will monitor behaviors to make sure those values are supported.

Customer and supplier surveys are another vital source of values information. These business partners can provide accurate feedback on how the organization demonstrates values such as Customer Orientation, Innovation, Continuous Improvement, and Collaboration. Their insights can verify that an organization is on course—or shatter its carefully cultivated illusions.

Culture: The Tie That Binds

An organization's quest to realize its vision revolves around achieving its critical success factors and living its values. This strategic focus will become the soul of the organization. It will play a major role in employee retention and performance, particularly during a time when the organization is in a state of flux and can't offer long-term job security—and when employees feel no obligation to demonstrate loyalty. If properly nurtured, culture allies people at all levels by instilling in them this shared set of values. It also conveys to employees what is expected of them and what they should expect of others.

False starts are common when dealing with vision, critical success factors, and values. One might be mistaken for another. Values, such as teamwork or empowerment, are sometimes mislabeled as CSFs. Systems improvement ideas, such as pay for performance and better communication, are also erroneously called CSFs. Quality often shows up as a critical success factor *and* a value. From a process or product point of view, quality *is* a CSF, as in *Continuously improve product quality.* From a behavioral point of view, it's a value, as in *People focusing on ways to improve quality.*

In other words, it will take some time, some thought, and some missteps before a strategic focus finally becomes a solid foundation for change. But the individual components of a strategic focus, whatever they might be for a particular organization, define where that organization needs to go and how it plans to get there. They are also key to restructuring and realigning the organization's systems and processes as it proceeds with the change effort.

CHAPTER 6

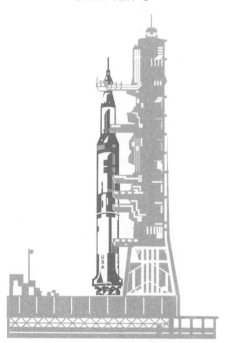

USING FOUR THRUSTS TO
ALIGN AN ORGANIZATION

S o far this discussion of change has addressed the first phase of the value-driven change process—creating a strategic focus for the change, using a vision, critical success factors, and values that reflect an organization's history, present state, and future direction. Now, with this phase completed, planning the change can move to phases two and three: design and implementation through high involvement. At this point, an organization looks at its processes and systems to determine which reinforce appropriate behaviors and which inhibit them. The aim is to leverage processes and systems that drive appropriate behaviors and realign those that stand as barriers. Examination of the four thrusts—communication, accountability, skills, and processes and systems—provides a framework for identifying alignment opportunities.

An organizational thrust narrows the context for looking at a system and acts as a magnifying glass for scrutinizing a particular aspect of the organization. Approaching the many issues involved in organizational change in this way helps to integrate and strengthen the four thrusts, which maintain the course and speed of the change effort.

Looking at a schematic of the Apollo spacecraft might be a good way to illustrate the concept of organizational thrusts. The following illustration shows that the engineers who designed Apollo placed a cluster of rockets at each 90-degree interval of the circumference of the command module. Located at four points on the fuselage—with each cluster containing four rockets positioned north, south, east, and west—the thrusters could be fired in any direction to alter the speed and course of the craft, allowing maximum maneuverability. This same theory applies to organizational thrusts. Energy focused in any one of the four thrusts, or in a combination of them, can alter the speed and course of a value-driven change.

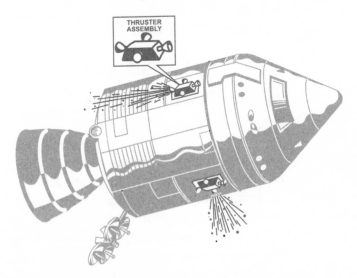

Figure 14. Focusing Energy: Aligning the Four Thrusts

The Importance of Alignment

If aligned and fine-tuned, the thrusts can drive and support a change effort, establish appropriate behaviors, and keep the effort on course.   Using and managing the thrusts is similar to Michael Collins' piloting of the Apollo 11 command module. When Collins found that the craft had strayed a hair off course during the mission, he activated its thrusters. Firing 2 of the 16 positional rockets for only a half second might have been enough to correct the course.

Such dexterity and control translate perfectly to this stage of the organizational change effort. To maintain course, various aspects of organizational systems require adjustment at certain times. Some require extreme levels of attention. Others do not.

At this stage, managing organizational change becomes an art, much like Collins' deft piloting of the Apollo 11 command module to the moon. Collins used a sophisticated control panel. An organization's leaders examine specific factors within the thrusts, not only to adjust processes and systems, but to encourage desired behaviors and discourage unwanted behaviors. This is an ideal way to support people who are living the organization's values and achieving its critical success factors.

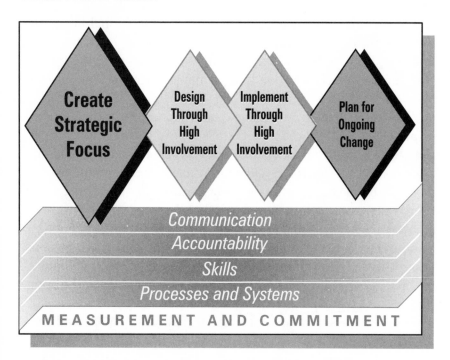

Figure 15. Value-Driven Change Model: Four Thrusts of Change

Overview of the Four Thrusts

The first thrust, *communication,* includes official releases of information through newsletters, brochures, formal meetings, and memos. It also involves organizational symbols and rituals, leadership behaviors, and the grapevine.

The second thrust, *accountability,* encompasses the areas of an organization's structure and performance management issues, such as clarifying expectations, providing coaching, and tracking progress. The accountability thrust directly links the workforce with the strategic focus, ensuring that people are living the values as they perform their jobs and, consequently, working to accomplish key business initiatives.

New behaviors often require new *skills,* the third thrust. This thrust includes technical skills related to the job, interactive or relationship skills, process improvement skills for taking action to make the organization better, business knowledge to build an understanding of the organization's position in the marketplace, and leadership skills needed to develop organizational talent and produce results. A value-driven change process identifies skills that support new behaviors and values, assesses people's current skill levels, and creates and implements effective training and development plans.

The fourth thrust, *processes and systems,* comprises the sequence of activities and procedures people follow to accomplish work (processes) and the policies that guide decision making within the organization (systems). Systems that need attention and realignment during a change effort vary from company to company. All companies must align three of the thrusts—communication, accountability, and skills. These three involve systems that need to be addressed early in the culture-change process for two reasons: first, because they communicate the direction and expectations of the change, and second, because they clarify the roles and responsibilities of the people involved in the effort.

The processes and systems thrust also helps address processes—manufacturing a product, providing a service, purchasing, tracking complaints, and invoicing—and systems—compensation, selection, and information management. Because processes and systems affect behavior, implementing a value-driven change most likely will involve improving, redesigning, or reengineering various processes and systems to encourage behavior that supports organizational values.

Tailoring the Four Thrusts

To be most effective, organizations should implement the entire value-driven change process in the sequence depicted in the process model. However, the order in which thrusts are analyzed and strengthened depends on an organization's strategic focus.

One insurance company had an objective to *Improve the cycle time for approving applications.* This insurance company determined that achieving such an objective required that processing clerks have more decision-making authority. The company's leaders launched their organizational change by moving toward self-directed teams within the accountability thrust. They followed up by taking action within the skills and communication thrusts. They also addressed the promotion, recognition, and compensation systems and the claims adjusting and underwriting processes.

Another organization used training in marketplace issues to build a strong case for change. As preparation for its change, a third organization spent a year focusing on leadership behaviors.

Approaching the thrusts with an eye to an organization's unique structure makes an excellent foundation for thinking through the culture change and creating a plan that fits a specific business situation. As an example, an organization might modify its performance management system to provide everyone with feedback on how well they live the new values. If handled properly, this accountability action:

- Aligns the performance management system with the new values.
- Communicates a strong message about what's important to the organization.
- Supports new skills required to live the values.
- Clarifies accountability.
- Strengthens the communication and skills thrusts.

These overlapping thrusts can constitute both the framework for and the results of organizational change.

The next four chapters detail organizational thrusts in a way that is meant to ignite the thought process for using the four thrusts to support all types of change efforts. Handling them correctly can support and even drive a change effort while maintaining an organization's unique personality and creating a nourishing work environment and ethic.

CHAPTER 7

COMMUNICATION

I t was the beginning of May 1961. Three weeks earlier, Soviet cosmonaut Yuri Gagarin had become the first man in space. Two weeks earlier, the invasion of Cuba by a group of exiles had ended bloodily at the Bay of Pigs. One week earlier, an Atlas booster rocket carrying an unmanned Mercury capsule had drifted off course and self-destructed. Four days earlier, a second Mercury test flight had exploded after liftoff.

In the wake of these disasters, John F. Kennedy faced the task of rallying his people. Despite the setbacks, he wanted to make America a "space-faring nation." He knew the fledgling NASA could not overtake the Soviets in a matter of a few months or even a few years. He needed a goal with a built-in cushion of time— time to catch up to and overtake the competition. Because no one could reach the moon in less than seven or eight years, this goal became the focal point of his vision to *explore new frontiers.*

Rallying the troops became a matter of communicating this goal to a country that had seen its national pride slowly erode following World War II. Before Congress, Kennedy stated:

> I believe this nation should commit itself to achieving the goal, before the decade is out, of landing a man on the moon and returning him safely to earth. No single space project in this period will be more impressive to mankind, or more important for the long-range exploration of space, and none will be so difficult or expensive to accomplish.

In a few sentences Kennedy communicated the goal, the actions needed to reach it, the costs and the difficulty, and the potential rewards. Within a decade the 400,000 technicians, engineers, and contractors working with NASA had successfully reached Kennedy's goal. They had heard him loud and clear.

Just as Kennedy conveyed his new-frontier initiative, the leaders of any organization can impart a new business and culture direction to the workforce through the *communication thrust.* This thrust encompasses formal communications, symbols and rituals, leadership behavior, and the grapevine.

The purpose of using the communication thrust is first to implant the thought, *This is where we're going. Do you want to come along?* The goal is to motivate people to both understand and support the organization's new direction. The communication thrust then does much more. It sets expectations for the organization as a whole, seeks and fosters enthusiasm and commitment, asks for involvement, and recognizes and reinforces appropriate behavior.

Communication is involved in every organizational event and action. This fact makes clear the importance—and the challenge—of managing and strengthening the communication thrust. Yet few organizations realize or effectively use the power of internal communication to foster a collective understanding. Usually their visions become part of a public relations campaign—and that's it. The vision sits as a vapid, emotionless collection of words rather than an inspirational rallying point for change.

On the other hand, a vision gains power exponentially when leadership communicates it in a way that everyone in the organization can understand. When this happens, it's possible for people to accept both the rationale for change and their roles in the new organization. Using the communication thrust's full complement of tools—formal communications, symbols and rituals, and leadership behavior—will develop a strong, commonly shared understanding of the vision.

Formal Communication

Organizations formally communicate with employees in a variety of ways. Many hold town meetings. More publish a monthly or quarterly newsletter. Many feature yearly state-of-the-business addresses by the CEO. Most distribute memos and post notices on bulletin boards. And some organizations even communicate business plans and targets, set by vice presidents to middle managers, to frontline supervisors and the rank and file.

However, for the majority of these organizations the greatest challenge is breathing life into such communications. For a workforce that has been distanced from senior leadership, formal communications concerning a new culture might appear to be advertisements rather than vehicles for giving them information, reinforcement, support, and encouragement in times of change. How does this happen? Taking a look at the approach of a major industrial manufacturing organization might help answer this question.

When leaders at one organization decided they needed a culture change that would improve their image with customers, they called in a communications consulting firm. Several well-intentioned consultants flew in, sat in on meetings, and listened to the customer-focused vision of senior leadership. They then caucused, devised some slogans, and imprinted them on everything from mugs to umbrellas.

For all their trouble, all their time and effort, and all the money spent on consultants and souvenirs, senior leaders at this industrial giant had created a new *program,* a very attractive advertising campaign to win over their own people.

With the same good intentions, management throughout the company implemented the program. Mugs, pins, and posters appeared everywhere within the company, and yet the customer-focused program failed to make its way into the fabric of the organization. Instead, resistance to the program grew.

It happens all too often. Employees have been led down this formal communication path before. In fact, they burn out on *programs.* So, hundreds of hours and thousands of dollars later, everyone uses the souvenirs. They smile and joke about all the customer-friendly propaganda. They still feel miles away from company executives, whom they rarely see. And nothing changes.

An organization that relies only on its formal system to communicate a culture change likely will achieve the same lackluster results. It might even hinder the change effort. Our society is inexorably drawn to advertising, yet views it with skepticism. If this is the case, why would an organization use a formal communication vehicle to advertise its way into a culture change? By delivering a message that an organization doesn't truly *live,* leaders do nothing but widen the credibility gap between themselves and the workforce.

Formal communication can't be used as the sole means of introducing and managing change. Instead, it must focus on the effort involved and recognize people who live the values in their day-to-day activities. Presenting examples of coworkers involved in actual activities and doing real work inspires employees. Academically extolling the virtues of teamwork does not. The effectiveness of communication also is directly related to the language of the message. It must be language that people at all levels of the organization can understand.

A chemical company that added a *Values in Action* column to its in-house newsletter provides a perfect real-life example. A feature on the company's Empowerment value recounted the formation of five project teams from the maintenance, engineering, and operations areas. These teams planned the scope of their work as well as their work schedules—tasks that had been the responsibility of plant management. The new teams met directly with vendors, received and approved work bids, and managed project vendors.

As a result, the project teams and vendors became strong partners, with several vendors commenting favorably about both team members and the company. The article concluded: "Empowering colleagues to develop, plan, manage, and complete these projects formed an atmosphere of teamwork, trust, and team ownership."

What more inspiring example could an organization want? Used to spotlight *progress* rather than talk about what *ought to be done,* effective communication vehicles target specific individual or team efforts. Regular columns like the one just cited change the message from a one-time gimmick to very specific recognition for an ongoing effort.

LaRoche Industries Inc., of Atlanta, Georgia, held a communication strategies session with 20 participants who represented different areas of the organization. This group brainstormed new and creative ideas to communicate to all associates information that would support LaRoche's vision, values, and critical success factors.

The ideas they came up with showed real ingenuity. One called for establishing an annual product fair that would travel to all LaRoche sites to demonstrate products, facilities, people, markets, and future plans. A second would provide associates with summaries of key reports—safety, environmental, financial, and customer surveys/complaints. A third was to publish a monthly *value calendar* of famous people to emphasize that living the values can produce excellence. Several of these ingenious ideas became a part of the communication team's overall plan.

Formal communication vehicles can also play a part in conveying critical success factors that involve teamwork, innovation, or process improvement. A large auto manufacturer wanted to find better ways to recognize team performance. Someone decided to install large video monitors in the cafeteria to show two- to five-minute video clips featuring different teams describing work problems and their solutions for those problems. On any given day workers and guests at the plant saw on video three or four frontline employees explaining various problems and demonstrating solutions. The videos not only recognized teams but also enabled people closest to the job to share their good ideas.

As the flow of information increases along formal lines of communication, some of that information will begin to flow upward—from the workforce to senior leadership. In the past many leaders solicited anonymous letters or used a suggestion box to collect employee feedback. Such methods imply that the only way people can give candid feedback is to cloak it in secrecy. On the other hand, seeking honest feedback through open, formal lines of communication builds trust.

One organization introduced project teams in its engineering and marketing departments. A general manager wanted to know how well these teams were functioning, so he convened a 10-member focus group from the two departments. The immediate feedback he received enabled him to take appropriate action to support the teams and increase their effectiveness.

This type of upward communication is an excellent way to measure the vision. Senior leadership definitely knows what it wants to achieve and *thinks* it knows what has been communicated. Upward communication allows leadership to learn what people actually are hearing and understanding—information that's invaluable for a successful change effort.

Rituals and Symbols

Rituals are ingrained ways of doing things, and people usually use them to celebrate success and communicate bad news. Meetings and new employee orientations fall in the category of organizational rituals. Meetings constitute the stage on which the drama of corporate values plays out. They're the most common and important organizational rituals.

Not quite a part of formal communication, the spontaneity of meetings enhances their credibility as a communication channel for values. Some meeting participants speak their minds, contribute, and model the values. Others watch the play and absorb the messages that convey what is important and what is not. Some meeting participants dissect the ritual in hushed hallway meetings or in the cafeteria: "Joe sure played with the facts in there," or "I can't believe Mary's openness. She really took some risks."

Meetings send important symbolic messages. Their effectiveness and the manner in which people conduct them—how they are opened, led, and closed—reflect an organization's culture and its leadership. The way meeting members handle conflict, their openness in exchanging ideas, and their follow-through on action items all gauge the health of the organization's values.

Robert Galvin, former CEO of Motorola, changed the order in which topics were discussed at monthly executive meetings, moving quality to the head of the agenda. The new agenda committed the first two hours of every meeting to quality improvement results, with other agenda items following. The rationale: As a key business driver, quality comes first. This small change sent an obvious message about Motorola's priorities and its driving value.

Symbols, like country club memberships, company cars, and executive dining rooms, permeate organizations and can represent an employee's status within the company. They grab people's attention. They generate respect and envy. Who gets an assigned parking space? Where do people eat? Who is salaried, and who is hourly? Who gets an office? An office with or without artwork? Who works at a metal desk, and who gets wood? Who needs a doctor's excuse for an absence, and more importantly, who doesn't? These seemingly minor issues serve as powerful symbols that can undermine the most well-intentioned value structures.

The language that organizations use can be powerful as well. The Weiler Corporation, a manufacturer in eastern Pennsylvania, has been looking at the various aspects of corporate language for years, making constant improvements to eliminate the line between haves and have-nots.

Signs in Weiler's parking lot show only the following types of parking: visitor, coworkers, safety coworker of the month, and disabled. It renamed its grievance procedure *disagreements*. New coworkers no longer begin *on probation*. Rather, they're in the *getting-to-know-each-other phase of employment*. It renamed the first, second, and third shifts the *day, evening,* and *night* shifts in an attempt to do away with the class connotation of the old names.

At one time Weiler's plant introduced *cellular manufacturing* by positioning employees in work cells. Thanks to the environment of open communication and feedback, the employees were able to say, "We don't like the word *cell*. It sounds too much like jail. And we don't consider our work to be like jail." The coworkers selected a new term: *work centers*. Simple change; powerful message.

Another manufacturing organization, this one based in Dallas, addressed similar language issues, this time dealing with three reserved parking spaces in front of the building—one for the plant manager and two for superintendents. Employees felt that this arrangement contradicted their value of Teamwork and took the issue to the quality steering committee. The committee decided to redesign the parking spots as an outdoor break area. They set aside money and encouraged teams to become involved in planning the redesign.

This project also became a skill practice in one of the organization's team training programs. After reaching consensus on the design, the teams used the money the committee set aside to buy a fence, picnic table, umbrella, and plants. The plant manager and superintendents, who are of course welcome to use the picnic area, now park their cars in the plant parking lot—just like everybody else.

Rituals and symbols are better understood at lower levels of the organization, where fewer perks exist. At higher levels many rituals and symbols are taken for granted or simply not recognized. Identifying and then aligning—or if necessary eliminating—rituals and symbols that don't support the values, build employee involvement in the change effort.

Communication and the Behavior of Leaders

An organization's strongest and most influential messages emanate from its most powerful people—leaders. Do these messages indicate that leaders are living the values? Are they acting as part of the corporate team? Do they walk the talk? Are they involving employees in making and implementing decisions? Are their decisions helping to achieve customer satisfaction?

Because of their power, leaders pave the way to involvement at various levels within the organization. Their behavior, if consistently positive, reflects a commitment to organizational values. Even something that seems insignificant, like being on time for meetings, shows people that leaders care enough to respect their time.

This respect then becomes a two-way street. Businessman James Cash Penney based his customer service policy on his Baptist upbringing and held employees to a high moral standard. However, he called employees his "associates" and gave store managers, most of whom started as sales clerks, one-third partnerships in their stores.

Penney was also well known as a teetotaler and demonstrated this behavior in his organization. Out of deference to this dynamic leader, J.C. Penney associates refrained from using alcohol at company-related events—not only during the years when Mr. Penney was active, but long after his retirement. Such respect for a leader—during working hours and after them as well—testifies to the way in which a leader's behavior permeates an organization and how employees emulate it.

The director of a veterans' affairs medical center in Texas wanted to schedule total quality training in a way that reinforced its message and importance. Training hospital staff is always difficult because staff members work around the clock, and training often means coming in during their *off* time. The center's first step took training to the employees.

The hospital scheduled training to support all shifts, including a session that started at 2:00 a.m. The director further reinforced the message of the training by kicking off this middle-of-the-night employee program, then staying to answer questions afterward. The director's presence said as much about the hospital's commitment to change as did the program material.

As part of a culture-change process, the president of Mott's USA (a division of Cadbury Beverages, Inc.) conducted all employee meetings to support the company's change implementation. These talks covered the company's past, present, and future. The president's consistent message communicated a clear understanding of the change and conveyed the commitment of Mott's leadership.

When leaders' behavior contradicts organizational values, it negates virtually everything an organization does or intends to do in a change effort. A large financial institution wanted to create a more empowered environment to achieve higher levels of customer satisfaction. More than 90 managers from around the country attended a session on high-performance work systems and their effect on leadership style. During the session the senior leader responsible for the entire event repeatedly stepped out of the meeting. Finally a consultant approached him to ask if anything was wrong. The consultant expressed concern about the message the leader's behavior sent to session participants. He assured the consultant that no one even noticed his frequent departures.

As part of that session's strategy, the consulting team collected questions from participants and announced that all questions would be answered by the end of the session. As questions were categorized by issue, the consultants discovered that more than 70 had been submitted to the senior leadership team. More than 50 of those dealt with the senior leader's frequent departures from the session. Given the time and expense of the session, participants failed to understand why their leader couldn't stay to hear the message. The leader had no idea how his behavior affected the group.

Then there is Jack Welch, CEO of General Electric, who in 1996 was named in *IndustryWeek*'s 25th annual CEO survey as "Most Respected CEO" for the third time in four years. He is the antithesis of the remote and untouchable leader. At the GE leadership development facility in Crotonville, New York, Welch spends hours working with his company's new leaders on ethics and responsibility issues. Welch's approach and attitude are reflected in his ability to greet hundreds of employees by name, review the performance of 500 general managers, and play a major role in compensation for GE senior executives.

In rare instances leaders demonstrate values that influence the workforce beyond the corporate realm and that translate into actions of true social significance. John T. Dillon, International Paper Company's chairman of the board and chief executive officer, is such a leader. In response to the burning of African-American churches in the Southern United States during 1993–95, Dillon donated all the materials needed to rebuild these destroyed churches. This gesture not only overjoyed parishioners, it inspired International Paper employees to help as well. Their internal fund-raising effort netted $40,000 in cash for the reconstruction—an amount the company then matched. Dillon's exceptional behavior and his employees' response illustrate the power and influence leaders can have within their own companies.

Informal Communication and the Grapevine

Every organization develops its own whispered, unofficial communication line that purports to convey the *real* story. No matter what his or her position in the organization, everyone participates in one way or another, whether standing around the water cooler or the golf tee. Such forms of unofficial communication aren't new—imagine the rumors that circulated within the Roman legions about their emperors. For thousands of years, the grapevine has thrived like a bad weed. In the Navy it's "scuttlebutt." In the corporate world it's the "rumor mill." It exists wherever people perceive a lack of information.

The grapevine becomes particularly important when an organization's formal communication process breaks down and when meetings don't deal with real issues. In these situations the grapevine provides the only source of real news, or at least what people perceive as real. In fact, much of the grapevine's information is and always has been based on speculation. The grapevine can be truly harmful when it proves to be the sole source of credible information because the implication then is that secrets are true and formal communications are not.

Leaders, however, should not be apprehensive about listening to the grapevine because it often identifies concerns that need to be addressed openly. Leaders can send a strong message about organizational communication by frankly discussing rumors at a team meeting. Even if the message is one people don't want to hear, leadership's open communication can build trust in a situation that has been eroded by rumors. Because the grapevine will never be eliminated, the goal of senior leadership should be to make it accurate. An effective communication strategy can help accomplish that goal.

Communication and Related Systems Alignment Issues

Leaders should view all organizational systems as potential communication vehicles. Systems such as compensation, promotion, and recognition all send consistent messages about accepted behaviors when they are aligned with the organizational values—and mixed messages when not aligned.

For example, the *compensation* system rewards accepted behaviors with raises and discourages unacceptable behaviors with lower-than-average or no increases. If an organization were to reward sales associates for new accounts rather than for client retention, it would send the message that landing new accounts is more important than retaining established ones. In the same vein, if a plant rewards managers for production and not for quality, then those managers naturally will set their sights on production goals, and quality might suffer.

Promotion systems communicate acceptable behavior in the same way. Perhaps an organization is striving to improve teamwork and cooperation; then someone fails to live the new values by sacrificing teamwork to achieve results. The organization can derail the effort if it overlooks the lack of teamwork and promotes the person because of the results. If this were to happen, the communicated message would be that teamwork really isn't important, that it's no more than office propaganda.

One swift, ill-conceived move could place an entire change effort in jeopardy. With this in mind, an organization can determine how to align a particular system with the strategic focus by asking the question, "What is this system communicating about our values?"

Recognition systems carry the power to convey vision and values, yet many organizations overlook this power. Some that do use recognition systems have shifted their focus from *employee-of-the-month* systems, which tend to lose credibility over time, to systems in which peers as well as leaders recognize one another. Recognition should be an attractive option for leaders because it rewards behaviors that live the vision and values, and does so at a modest cost. Used properly, recognition can spice up the workplace.

DDI awards "STARs" as a form of recognition. **STAR** is an acronym for a specific, challenging **S**ituation or **T**ask, the **A**ctions an associate takes to deal with the situation, and the **R**esults those actions achieve. STARs spontaneously awarded by peers to other peers can mean as much as a plaque or a handshake from senior leadership. STARs also support DDI's Teamwork value. Figure 16 depicts a commonly used STAR form.

Concepts such as STARs help senior leadership communicate values to each person in the organization. Used collectively, communication systems convey the new direction and secure employee commitment. The next step involves helping those employees understand their roles and responsibilities within the organization. Roles and responsibilities are the key to accountability and to synchronizing all four thrusts.

a STAR regarding . . .

Situation or **T**ask

Action

Result

Recorded by:
CC:

Figure 16. STAR form

CHAPTER 8

ACCOUNTABILITY

☆ ☆ ☆

In the dry world of dictionaries, accountability means "having the obligation to report, explain, or justify something . . . answerable for something within one's power or control." In the rich and dynamic world of work, the word also implies a deep commitment to getting things done and a personal ownership in making sure they are done well.

Achieving change in an organization requires clear accountability at every level. Employees at all levels need to *feel* accountable and must be *held* accountable for both what they achieve and how they achieve it. This can happen only if objectives align with critical success factors and if behaviors align with values.

This chapter explores how to achieve this degree of accountability by using an effective performance management system and the structure of the organization itself. With performance management, building a culture that drives business strategy means seeking a balanced emphasis on both quantifiable objectives and behavioral expectations. Building a competitive culture also might involve addressing traditional organizational structures and configurations that no longer work.

Accountability and Performance Management

Once senior leaders have set a clear direction and developed a vision for the organization, they face their toughest challenges: driving the change throughout the organization, facing the ramifications, and securing a commitment to the new direction from every employee. For as much bad press as performance management has received, strong performance management systems can be the most effective tool for driving a change effort and achieving optimal organizational performance. An effective performance management system also provides role clarity and accountabilities for the entire organization.

Accountability tells employees when they're up to bat. Without it, they don't know when to swing. It directs people's energy and focus toward critical organizational issues. If designed and implemented correctly, performance management systems establish role clarity—from senior levels to each associate in the organization—so that everyone knows how to contribute to the organization's goals and objectives.

An effective performance management system is the best management tool available to senior executives whose job is to focus energy on key issues and create clear accountabilities for those issues. This only works, however, if the system focuses on *both* the business and the culture strategies.

The leaders of a midsize British pharmaceutical company wanted to implement their newly created vision to more effectively focus on key factors for success. Their solution was to put in place a performance management system that would move the organization rapidly forward. The company's senior executive team began the implementation by:

1. Establishing concrete measures for the vision and critical success factors (speed to market, production efficiency, and brand recognition).

2. Charging each member of the team with developing individual key result areas and objectives, then sharing

them with the entire team in order to clarify roles and accountabilities.

3. Agreeing on implementation and communication actions.
4. Cascading the driving accountabilities and objectives throughout the organization.

This process produced:

- A scorecard to measure key organizational success factors that the senior team could track on a quarterly basis. (Note: The measures for the key factors or critical success factors are lead indicators of performance rather than lag indicators. See Chapter 2 for more discussion on lead and lag indicators.)

- For the first time, clear accountabilities at the senior level, along with role clarity for senior executives regarding each key factor.

- Clear performance plans for all senior executives that could cascade to all employees through divisions and departments.

- Buy-in, at the top, that this management process was a way to manage the business, not just a human resource or administrative system for managing compensation.

The dynamic Milton Hershey School for underprivileged children in Hershey, Pennsylvania, implemented a similar "conversion." The school's visionary CEO and senior leadership team developed a broad, aggressive, five-year strategic plan. Introducing a performance management system helped them translate the strategic plan into clear accountabilities. The system's measurement methods clarified roles and focused senior team members on the critical actions that would need attention in the coming five years.

In a major change effort, establishing clear accountabilities is critical—but it's not the only action needed. Leadership must also gain people's involvement and commitment to the new culture. A new set of values will require learning and reinforcing behaviors that will support the new culture strategy. And during change, employee disorientation could be at an all-time high, while morale and job satisfaction might hit an all-time low.

The performance management system, therefore, must drive not only the *whats*, or outputs, but also the *hows*—the behaviors that produce a culture that enhances and supports the vision and guides people while they work to achieve the business strategy. For example, if *Increasing customer loyalty and retention* is a critical success factor, associates must have the support and tools to behave in a way that demonstrates high customer orientation, high levels of service skills, and flexibility to meet customer needs on the spot—without multiple levels of approval.

Commonly Shared Values' Role in Performance Management

Most senior leaders believe that employees understand the *whats*. They also believe that employees are using measurement methods to track their own performance. But these same leaders would identify driving the organization's culture as one of the greatest and most critical challenges they face.

Scores of acclaimed leaders attest to the importance of managing an organization's culture. Among them are Jack Welch of General Electric, Jan Carlzon of Scandinavian Airline Systems, George Fisher of Eastman Kodak, Fred Smith of Federal Express, and Ray Gilmartin of Merck and Company, Inc. Authors such as John Kotter, Warren Bennis, William C. Byham, Edward Lawler III, and Stephen Covey, also underscore the criticality of effectively managing culture.

A set of commonly shared values, such as Teamwork, Innovation, Process Improvement, Meeting Customer Needs, and Care for People, translates into behaviors that hold all associates accountable for how they do their jobs, just as they would measure the objectives they achieve. This drives behavior in support of a culture that is clearly aligned with the key objectives and the vision of the organization.

Expectations and feedback in many areas can transform an organization's values from theory into daily reality. Figure 17 shows how values can be demonstrated in both quantitative objectives and behavioral expectations. Setting behavioral expectations isn't necessarily a difficult task for leaders, particularly if they have defined core values/competencies that the organization must demonstrate to achieve success. The difficult task is coaching and providing feedback on the behaviors. Grouping similar behaviors into categories (dimensions or competencies) can narrow the list down to the best five to seven key dimensions that will reflect the values and help people achieve key objectives or goals.

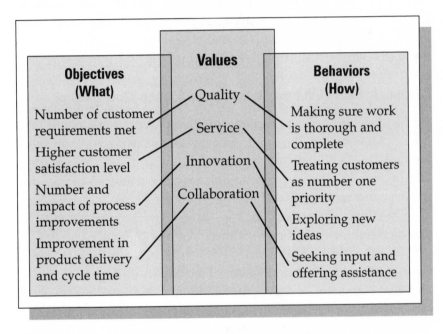

Figure 17. Relationship of Values, Objectives, and Behaviors

Effective Performance Management Systems

In 1993 Development Dimensions International teamed with the Society for Human Resource Management to conduct a nation-wide research study on performance management systems. This study highlighted the corporate community's frustrations with many performance management systems. Most organizations change their systems every four or five years because they're dissatisfied with some aspects of the approach. However, in some organizations a system can thrive and serve as the effective management tool it was always intended to be.

What differentiates one performance system from another? What makes one work while another fails? Performance management systems that work effectively over a long period of time meet the following criteria:

The System Covers Objectives and Behaviors

The system covers both the *whats* (objectives) and the *hows* (behaviors). To better steer and shape performance, the system should involve setting expectations for progress, coaching, giving feedback on progress, and measuring progress in both objectives and behaviors.

The System Links to the Strategic Focus

The system links accountabilities (objectives and behaviors) to the organization's strategies, vision, critical success factors, and values. Without this tie to the big picture, it's almost impossible to gain the appropriate level of commitment to the vision and make people feel that they have a key role in achieving that vision.

The System Focuses on Process

The system must focus on process rather than on form or paperwork. Real performance management involves far more than setting goals at the beginning of a business year and reviewing performance at the end of that year. It's a continuous process of coaching and providing feedback throughout the year.

The System Inspires Employee Commitment

Employee commitment to the new system is essential. This level of buy-in occurs when employees feel a sense of ownership because they're involved in implementing the system—they participate in setting their objectives and behavioral expectations, possess the ability to track their own performance, and attend (or even request) periodic coaching sessions. Employees should also measure their performance before their supervisor does. This high-involvement approach to performance management dramatically increases employee job satisfaction and ownership of the process.

The System Involves Continuous Monitoring

The system must look forward as much as it looks back. Evaluating past performance is part of the process; however, if coaching and feedback take place continuously during the business cycle, the year-end review should be a positive, productive discussion. The discussion should focus on future development in improving performance levels or preparing for increased responsibility. This review should be a cakewalk for managers because employees lead the discussion of performance in relation to the performance plan and also take the lead in ratings. Managers, therefore, can focus on the future and future development—a much easier task than waging a running battle over ratings.

The System Includes Performance Management Training

Organizations must conduct mandatory performance management training for all employees who use the system. All leaders, even the CEO, should receive how-to training regarding behavioral expectations and setting objectives, tracking and evaluating performance, and coaching and providing feedback. These skills *do not* automatically come with the title of supervisor, manager, vice president, or CEO. Anyone who uses the system needs training in how to set objectives and behavioral expectations, how to track and evaluate performance, and how to receive feedback and coaching in a way that helps improve performance.

The System Must Drive the Culture and Business Strategies

Performance management must be perceived as a line management system used to drive and manage the business, not as an HR compensation system. Logic links it to compensation because organizations should pay for performance (achieving both *whats* and *hows*). The level of performance documented by an effective system is one significant piece of data used for deciding compensation levels. But performance management's real power is in focusing energy and accountabilities on critical business issues. In fact, a senior line manager, preferably the CEO or COO, should be the champion of the system so everyone understands that it is a way of life in the organization.

The System Includes Self-Evaluation

A continuous improvement ethic can occur only within the context of a regular feedback loop and ongoing evaluation of the system's effectiveness. Therefore, to be effective, a performance management system must be designed to evaluate itself. There are many ways to evaluate the system, including surveys, focus groups, and random sampling of performance documentation. The key is to have a process that communicates what is working well and what needs to work better. The system is working efficiently if:

- Employees have a clear understanding of the strategic business plan and how their goals and objectives contribute to it.

- Employees have a say in establishing their objectives and behavioral expectations.

- Supervisors and managers see performance management as a way to ensure their unit's success.

- Supervisors and managers understand that their role is to ensure that employees achieve their objectives and behavioral expectations.

- The performance management system builds a sense of trust and partnership between supervisor and employee.

If the system hits these key points, then performance management will succeed in helping to drive any change the organization wants to make. It helps to bear in mind that it takes a few years to acclimate all employees to performance management so that they use the system effectively.

A performance management system can be applied to team structures as well as individuals. Team performance can be measured and tracked by integrating team objectives and practices to live the values. A dimension/competency design (mentioned previously) will capture individual contributions to the team. The more difficult aspect of team performance management is the feedback process, which can vary from a meeting of the team leader with each individual to a group process in which everyone provides feedback to the team members. The process will vary with the team's cohesiveness and maturity.

Accountability and Organizational Structure

Use of the term *organization* might lead to the assumption that organizations are or should be *organized*. Unfortunately, existing organizational structures, which can help or hinder employees in living the values, can easily create communication barriers that slow down work processes. An organization attempting to build a competitive culture faces the critical challenge of determining which type of organizational structure will minimize such communication and process barriers. Organizations exercise many structural options; however, the terms *vertical* and *horizontal* describe the two basic structural options.

Vertical Structures, Job Design, and Accountability

The term "vertical" denotes an organization designed around functions, with a hierarchical management structure. In his book *The Ultimate Advantage,* Edward E. Lawler III (1992) dates this control-oriented approach back to the late 19th century. At that time industrial engineer Frederick Winslow Taylor documented the concept of *scientific management,* which is based, according to Lawler, on the idea "that productivity is maximized when the work of low-level participants in an organization is specialized, standardized, and simplified. . . . Managers are the only ones who are expected to think, coordinate, and control" (p. 26). Lawler points out that while the term "scientific management" has become obscure, Taylor's concept still dominates organizational structures.

Although many organizations consider implementing alternative structures, a vertically structured organization need not translate into silos and bureaucracy. Even organizations with vertical structures can have minimum bureaucracy if they drive the appropriate behaviors. Leadership still should examine the structure to determine whether it enables people to live the values or whether it creates barriers to positive behavior. Cultural barriers embedded in the structure might be reflected in comments such as "throwing work over the wall" to another department or "It's not my job."

These types of barriers can be addressed without restructuring the entire organization. Examining and changing job design is the key. *Job design* is the work an individual accomplishes. A job, usually documented in a job description, can be designed to help an employee live the values.

For example, when tellers in a bank were given access to additional computer screens, it was easier for them to live the value of Customer Service because they found it easier to provide customers with needed information. An auto subassembly plant redesigned the work of engineers to assure that they could spend more time on the factory floor and with the marketing department. This change produced more customer-friendly designs and brought down the cultural walls between those areas of the organization. These employees eventually lost the sense that work was "being thrown over the walls" between departments.

At a major hotel, employees, rather than managers, began to make certain purchasing decisions. This simple move improved service and cycle time.

Some easy guidelines for designing jobs include:

- Make sure the work has variety, challenge, and meaning.
- Build authority and responsibility into the job.
- Adapt jobs to fit individual competency levels and motivations when possible.

New job designs require new skills. In the above examples the bank teller and employee making purchasing decisions probably needed new technical skills, while the engineer required additional interpersonal skills. Broadening jobs without providing the means to acquire necessary skills can frustrate employees and even lead to failure in their new assignments.

Looking at job design is critical to addressing cultural barriers in traditionally designed organizations. Typically, companies initiate the analysis because they need employees with more flexibility. The analysis itself often helps leaders understand and value a horizontally structured organization.

In her book *In the Age of the Smart Machine,* Shoshana Zuboff (1988) provides a reminder that one of the primary purposes of the traditional, hierarchical, vertically structured organization was to combine and refine information and pass it upward. She points out that although this purpose has been obviated by the computer, most organizational structures are still burdened with multiple layers of information-passing bureaucracy. Therefore, this increasing reliance on the computer by society in general, and business in particular, promotes a corresponding interest in horizontally structured organizations.

Horizontal Structures, Teams, and Accountability

The concept of the *horizontal* organization traces its history to what was once called *participative management.* Participative management eliminates identifying managers as *thinkers* and workers as *doers.* Its evolution gradually widened the concept of the horizontal organization. Only in the past decade, according to Lawler, "have writers been concerned with the broader organizational design and systems issues that arise when an entire organization is managed with the involvement-oriented approach" (p. 31). The horizontal organizational design is intended to deal with many of these issues.

The term *horizontal organization* was coined to reflect the horizontal flow of work processes. That is, considering the vertical design of most organizational charts, all work processes flow horizontally *across* the functions. This begs the question, "Why not find an organizational structure that helps this natural flow?" Horizontal organizations feature work groups configured around work processes. Instead of work being broken down into specialized, fragmented pieces, the work groups or teams are accountable for entire processes or large portions of it. They are also accountable for some of the problem solution and solution implementation responsibilities formerly reserved for managers.

The remainder of this chapter clarifies team "language" and touches on some of the key concepts behind the horizontal organization. When considering how to use structure to help an organization live its values, remember that all business imperfections do not stem from an organization's structure.

The horizontal team-based structure is not a solution for every business. This caution is based on the experience of many organizations that have multiple teams but minimal teamwork. If teamwork is a value deemed appropriate for the new culture and an organization wants employees to live this value, then people must be held accountable for behaviors exhibited on the job. A team structure can make this behavior easier to demonstrate, but it doesn't guarantee success. As many senior leaders have learned from personal experience, a teams structure without teamwork is really a structure of committees.

The ever-evolving language of teams can be confusing. The single word "team" is used to describe a range of structures. Asking the following questions helps to determine the best use of teams:

- Is the purpose of the team to maximize performance of daily work, to handle a special project, to take advantage of an improvement opportunity, or to solve a problem?
- Is the team's membership reflective of several functions (as in cross-functional), or do all team members represent the same function?
- Does membership include one level of the organization or a variety of levels?
- How does membership change?
- Is the tenure (or life) of the team permanent, or will it disband when the task is complete?

Figure 18 on page 88 simplifies team language and links commonly used terminology with team purpose, membership (including the amount of time members devote to the team), tenure, and examples. It describes team design but doesn't describe team behavior. Living the value of teamwork and being empowered to make decisions—not just recommendations—make team structures powerful. Any of the teams described in Figure 18 can be highly empowered or self-directed. Powerful, productive teams are clear on their accountabilities, know their boundaries, and are expected to take action.

Success stories of teamwork combined with empowerment are common. The key to success is holding teams accountable for results. Of course, it will take new skills to achieve positive results, just as it will take more communication, meetings, and the right reward systems. However, the main reason for teams is to achieve results, so team performance must be managed just as individual performance is managed. Teams need to know what is expected of them, and they need to receive feedback on progress.

Many organizations are overrun with ineffective teams. Clarifying accountabilities before team implementation and providing ongoing feedback on progress toward objectives—and on living the values—create a high probability that teams will achieve results.

Team	Purpose	Membership	Tenure	Example
Process Action Team (PAT)	Improve an entire process, identifying problems/ improvement opportunities. PAT then commissions a CAT.	Cross-functional, cross-level group; part time.	Permanent; membership can rotate as needed.	Analyzes manufacturing or order-fulfillment process.
Corrective Action Team (CAT)	Identify problem root cause and determine, implement, and monitor solution.	Cross-functional or functional; part time.	Temporary; disbands at problem resolution.	Eliminates variation in a drilling operation.
Quality Improvement Team (QIT)	Improve/ Correct processes/ problems within one function.	Small group from one functional area; part time; rotating.	Permanent; scheduled rotation of members.	Determines inventory process improvements, then addresses another issue (e.g., document-ation errors).
Task Force or Project Team	Accomplish stated mission.	Cross-functional or functional; part time or full time.	Temporary; disbands at problem resolution.	Missions range from plant start-up to safety improvements.
Natural Work Team	Accomplish daily work, making decisions and resolving issues.	All members from one function; full time.	Permanent; membership changes with job openings.	Welders, assemblers, or expediters.
Redesigned Work Team	Accomplish daily work, making decisions and resolving issues.	Cross-functional; full time.	Permanent; membership changes with job openings.	Cutters, welders, or painters.
Virtual Team or Organization	Operate as complete enterprise to accomplish specified task.	Members from many functional areas; could include customers/ vendors.	Temporary; disbands when task completed.	A product design team with members all over the world.

Figure 18. Team Structure: Purpose, Membership, and Tenure

Teams at the Miller Brewing Company's Trenton plant manage their own performance by setting yearly group goals that align with the organization's direction and by developing a group action plan. Feedback from one team member to another is ongoing, and the group as a whole handles yearly, face-to-face performance reviews. This ongoing feedback assures that there are no surprises. In this way, Miller sets expectations and reviews progress for individuals and for the teams they represent. Such a system strives to live the values while providing clear accountabilities and fostering ongoing progress toward achieving organizational objectives.

Clear accountabilities at every level of the organization provide channels for change as employees accept and understand both *what they achieve* and *how they achieve it*. Their objectives must align with CSFs, and their behaviors with the values. However, they must also possess the skills essential to support the systems and processes found in the new organization. The next chapter addresses the wide variety of skills and abilities that compose the skills thrust.

CHAPTER 9

SKILLS

The Apollo astronauts trained . . . and trained . . . and trained to be the first men on the moon. Astronomy, space aeronautics, physical conditioning, weightlessness training—all were part of their preparation to handle the unique environment of space. Similarly, employees in an organization undergoing change must acquire the skills they'll need to accompany the organization on its journey toward improvement.

A culture change requires that people take on new and additional responsibilities. Poor or unmatched skills can crash a change initiative and severely damage workforce commitment and involvement. Consider the following truisms about skills and learning.

There is a difference between awareness training and skills training. *Awareness training* informs people about a topic—perhaps the organization's competitive situation. The downside of awareness training is that too many change efforts rely on it exclusively. These organizations spend their entire budget on half- or full-day training sessions but fail to give the appropriate attention to behaviors.   Conversely, *skills training* creates the ability to perform a new technical, interactive, or team-related skill that's needed on a daily basis. Awareness training can make people more receptive to new skills, but only skills training leads directly to behavioral change.

People learn many skills outside formal training classes. In some development situations hands-on experience, such as participating in a task force or serving as a trainer, is more effective than classes or seminars.

There must be a need and a plan for learning. Skill development relies on several factors: a person's desire to change and to develop a skill, a diagnosis of the individual's current skill level, an effective learning process, and a way to track progress. Developing skills also requires an appropriate level of *learning tension*, that is, understanding of the critical value (immediate and long term) of the new skill set. Learning tension ensures that new skills will be acquired at the teachable moment, a point in time when the learner both wants and needs the skill.

Skill areas often overlap for any one job or role. Skill areas can include business knowledge, technical skills, interactive skills, continuous improvement skills, and leadership skills.   For example, customer service representatives might find product and process knowledge to be more vital to their jobs than interactive skills, such as handling irate customers. They could argue that customer needs are met by understanding the business, products, and processes. In reality, the skill sets overlap; everyone who deals with customers needs to possess business knowledge, technical skills, and interactive skills.

If an organization plans to shift to some level of involvement, leaders must help people develop in ways that will support that change effort.   This involves developing skills in all important areas, as outlined in the following sections.

Business Knowledge

An organization about to launch a change effort will enhance employee performance by sharing general background information about the organization's place in the industry in general and about its business in particular. Leaders are paying attention to the concept of an employee thinking like a business owner who is responsible for the success of the enterprise. People who have acquired this sense of "ownership" through knowledge of their company's business can more easily understand the relevance of their jobs to overall goals, the need for change, and the role of the new values in the change effort. Many organizations realize the importance of making employees aware of financial information, customer complaints, and competitive news. They convey this information regularly through the various communication channels described in Chapter 7.

Business knowledge becomes a powerful tool when sharing it is an ongoing process. Maytag Corporation held development sessions to educate assembly line workers about various aspects of the business. They used maps that graphically depicted various areas of the Maytag operation. These sessions, which detailed the company's competitive situation, revenue stream, and major processes, helped new and hourly employees understand Maytag's overall business, manufacturing processes, financing, cash flow, and competition. This type of awareness training helped employees understand how their jobs contributed to organizational success.

Technical Skills

Technical skills enable people to perform the primary tasks their jobs/roles require. A person's title or role usually defines these skills, such as *writing* and *editing* for a job title of *publications specialist*. Any change in a job or role must be accompanied by examining the technical skill area to determine whether the job and skill level match.

When levels of involvement change, people must invariably learn new skills as they expand the scope of their responsibilities. For example, if employees are empowered to make decisions and recommendations about the assembly line, they will need training that links process steps to productivity. If engineers are expected to price a project as well as design it, they will need skills in determining costs and calculating price and profit margins. Involving people in determining the skills they need to carry out their new and expanded responsibilities ensures that they'll get what they need to support the change effort and the organization's new direction.

Anglian Water, which supplies water and treats waste for the largest geographical area in the United Kingdom, shifted some management responsibilities to teams. The company supported that responsibility shift with training. Anglian gave a self-managing technician team the responsibility of handling sewage treatment in the Kesteven territory. Team members received training in a new range of skills that gave them the capability to handle tasks previously carried out by managers. These expanded responsibilities included inviting and then reviewing offers for building/construction work up to 30K (sterling) (U.S. $45,000) in each financial year, making decisions, communicating with the parties involved, and sanctioning work.

Interactive Skills

Interaction is the part of the work process that determines how work gets done. Interactive skills most directly link values to behaviors. If an organization emphasizes Teamwork as a value, then one of its measures of interactive behavior is based on building teamwork. Using workforce involvement to achieve change brings with it increased interactions among employees. Consequently, as involvement becomes more pervasive, it's essential to provide a means to improve interaction skills throughout the organization.

Blue Cross and Blue Shield of Montana experienced culture shock in the area of interactions. Says Jane DeLong, "There was a note that we found from a couple of years ago that said, 'If you have a question, don't ask your coworker, ask your supervisor.' There used to be a belief here that only supervisors had the right answers and that your coworkers were likely to give you the wrong ones. Since that change, there's definitely a lot of sharing with partners and coworkers."

Involvement also is a way of life at another insurer. In order to maintain the highest level of customer service, the Kemper Insurance Company reengineered work processes and moved to a team environment. These changes required a parallel change in the way leaders approached their new roles, including leading through vision and values, championing continuous improvement, building business partnerships, and facilitating learning.

Change leaders at Kemper used a top-down approach that started at the highest level in the organization. They began the culture change by providing all leaders with a multirater (360°) assessment of their current skill level and feedback that targeted each leader's strengths and developmental areas. These multirater assessments relied on feedback from the people who worked with these leaders. Following the assessments, Kemper provided the leaders with the knowledge and skills to function effectively in the reengineered environment.

Kemper's leaders use their new skills daily. In problem-solving discussions they speak a common language and more comfortably address trust issues by referring to them as *trust traps* and *trust strategies*. Some have passed this training on to their teams.

Kemper continues to use its top-down approach to leadership development and, as the culture change progresses, constantly looks for ways to support leaders in their new roles.

Perot Systems, the computer services and business transformation company, is using another leadership development approach. The organization breaks down leadership into categories: leaders of people, leaders of technology, leaders of content, thought leaders, and example setters. And to drive its change effort, Perot Systems requires every person in the organization to demonstrate leadership competence—regardless of level or position in the company. As the company undergoes change, it provides tools and support to all employees via intranet. This approach uses the latest technology to constantly reinforce leadership as a driver of change.

Every industry prizes interactive service skills because the quality of service sets an organization apart from its competition. Organizations that emphasize the value of customers are the same ones that encourage employees in areas such as manufacturing and engineering to meet the customer directly. Many organizations involved in process improvement efforts also expand the definition of *customer* to include internal partners.

In a highly competitive, demanding marketplace, it is imperative to scrutinize the manner in which employees meet the personal and practical needs of external and internal customers. Employees must have the skills required to deal with dissatisfied customers, then go one step further by actually *encouraging* customers to express their dissatisfaction. This approach alerts employees to problem areas that need to be addressed.

Lantech, Inc., packaging specialists, wanted to solicit better feedback from customers in order to increase customer satisfaction. The company assigned a resource team of eight people to improve areas that would help accomplish this goal. This customer satisfaction initiative not only collected valuable customer insight, it also effected internal processes and regenerated interest in all departments for better communication and interaction skills, higher levels of empowerment, and effective problem solving. The resource team succeeded because of its superior interaction skills. The team asked customers for information and then implemented improvement solutions. Interaction and teamwork were the keys to raising the level of customer satisfaction.

Process Improvement Skills

Process improvement skills should be available at all levels to address the driving business need of ever-increasing customer expectations—getting a *better* product or service and getting it *faster* and at a *lower cost.* Among these skills are the ability to assess a situation or issue, determine its causes, target ideas and solutions, and implement ongoing actions. These skills also involve using certain tools, such as cause-and-effect diagrams, run charts, and solution-implication diagrams.

The University of Cincinnati Medical Center needed to improve process efficiency throughout the organization to achieve a patient-focused culture. To develop an ethic and a system for improving operational efficiency, the medical center used a two-part approach. It trained 45 employees as process action team facilitators who, once trained, set up process action teams throughout the hospital to identify opportunities for improvement and make recommendations for changes. This major initiative provided process improvement skills to people throughout the facility.

In Buick Motor Division's customer-focused change effort, company and dealership employees received process improvement training to remove acknowledged barriers to customer satisfaction. Dealership employees used their new skills to improve processes in areas closest to the customer, including new car delivery and service-order write-ups. A complete analysis of the new car delivery process, followed by employees' process improvements, shifted the focus from completing administrative details to providing fun and excitement for the customer.

The laboratory service at a Midwestern hospital experienced difficulty in reporting STAT lab test results to the hospital's physicians in a timely manner. It was a barrier to achieving the hospital's vision of "partnerships for the patient." The lab determined that doctors often created the problem because they were unavailable. Lab staffers instituted two simple but effective improvements. They printed the results in the lab and sent them to the printer on the appropriate floor as well. Lab workers also requested permission for direct access to physicians' beepers to notify them when test results were ready. These process improvements quickly put the information in the hands of the people who needed it.

Leadership Skills

In cultures that use some aspect of employee involvement to achieve organizational change, leaders serve at various times as catalysts, coaches, mentors, and facilitators. They might also head cross-functional teams or task forces. All these roles involve leadership skills. As leaders take on such roles, they might find themselves spending more time clarifying boundaries and less time making final decisions—leaving some of those decisions to people closest to the customer. Effective leaders who want to nurture a spirit of involvement refrain from solving problems for employees. Rather, they ask questions that prompt people to analyze a situation and solve their own problems.

Leaders in culture-change environments focus their attention on making sure people understand how their roles in the change effort relate to the organization's strategic focus and to realizing its vision. They also focus on process efficiency, employee growth, and the accurate and timely communication of information.

A ball bearing plant wanted to move toward a high-performance environment. Realizing that the change would require a shift from a "supervisory" mind-set to the concept of leadership as a role, the company decided to implement the change in two phases. The first phase comprised a series of leadership training modules that would lay the foundation and prepare people for the change. The actual change implementation began in phase two.

For their organizational change, Carpenter Technology Corporation first trained supervisors then instituted regular meetings to discuss all issues related to the change effort. These meetings provided supervisors with the opportunity to discuss issues, change behaviors, and grow in their new roles.

Skills for the Future

The work demands of the next millennium will require employees who can step into leadership roles at any given time, serving as leaders of cross-functional and project teams as well as meeting facilitators and participants. New, expanded roles translate into a need for leadership skills in building partnerships between groups or departments within the organization, improving productivity, self-managing careers and development, dealing with ambiguity in the workplace, and managing people who work in virtual offices or on virtual teams. Increasingly, people also will need skills for working with diverse populations and demonstrating sensitivity to global perspectives and approaches.

Individuals in organizations of the future must possess a continuous learning ethic for two basic reasons: the inevitable and rapid advancement of technology and the changing nature of organizations. The process of identifying and acquiring new skills, therefore, never stops. Concurrently, as organizational cultures strengthen and capabilities broaden, employees will likely lose their resistance to learning. New skills then become an asset because they help align the skills thrust with the strategic focus. At this point, employees will see the positive effect enhanced skills have on their compensation and job security.

Even though they're armed with these new and enhanced skills, some organizations still do not achieve the results that leadership desires. If one believes Deming's philosophy—that most organizations' problems are process or systems issues—then it follows that skill enhancement alone will not solve such problems. The skills thrust, however, involves vitally important systems that, when aligned, will move the organization ahead in its quest for change.

CHAPTER 10

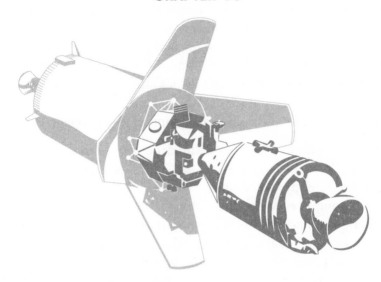

PROCESSES AND SYSTEMS

☆ ☆ ☆

The last verbal signal before a space launch is "All systems are go!" And they had better be. All navigation, propulsion, and telemetry systems must be aligned, synchronized, and ready to function, or the mission is scrapped. The historic flight of Apollo 11 depended on hundreds of systems—all aligned—all in go mode. An aligned system launched the Saturn 5 rocket. Another guided the command module to lunar orbit and the excursion module to the lunar surface. Another allowed communication to flow smoothly so that we could hear "The Eagle has landed" across a quarter of a million miles in space. Yet other systems sent data back to earth that would make future lunar exploration safer and more exact.

Aligned systems made the Apollo missions possible. They were as critical to the mission as aligned processes and systems are to a successful organizational change. The discussion that follows and those of the three previous chapters are based on the tenet that without system alignment, it's impossible to implement desired change. This chapter explores the fourth thrust—a grouping of processes and systems not previously addressed: selection, compensation, recognition, information management, career and development planning, job rotation, and promotion. The processes and systems thrust supports an organization's culture in strong yet subtle ways and influences both values and critical success factors.

Aligning Processes and Systems to Support the Strategic Focus

Processes often contain embedded behaviors that support the values or the critical success factors, such as a requirement that work must be signed as a mark of the value of *excellence*. Certain processes might even require behavior that actually discourages people from demonstrating desired values or achieving the CSFs. One can say then, that organizational and individual behaviors are a product of processes and systems. *Systems* guide decision making within organizations. During a change effort, systems must be aligned with both the business strategy and the culture strategy.

If an organization's business strategy requires a new culture, the only way to realize that culture is to analyze, modify if necessary, and realign processes and systems to drive behaviors related to the new culture's values. Teamwork is a prime example. Below is a short list of possible systems alignment questions relating to the Teamwork value. How an organization answers them will identify what *truly counts* in that organization.

- Does our organization hire or promote individuals based on their ability to participate in a team environment?
- Is the performance management system team based, or does it focus on individuals?
- Does our organization reward and recognize teams or individuals?
- Does compensation encourage cross-training and multi-skilling?
- Does our training system build the appropriate team-work and leadership skills?

Likewise, processes and systems must support not only the values but the key strategies or critical success factors as well.

This suggests a list of process alignment checks pertaining to a CSF such as *Reduce cycle time.* These issues might include:

- How does our organization manage conflict between the marketing and R&D departments in order to get products to market faster?

- Do our engineering and manufacturing areas share performance goals and work together as a team?

- How much empowerment is built into our customer-complaint resolution process to ensure we're responsive to customer needs?

- Does our information management system provide client operational information to the teams that need it?

Imagine the work involved in an alignment that touches all these systems—hiring, promotion, compensation, performance management, rewards and recognition, training—and this relates to the Teamwork value alone! Imagine the price to pay if a company doesn't support its values and eliminate the conflicting messages sent by unaligned systems.

Comparing processes and systems in terms of the significant impact they have on an organization's strategic focus helps to determine the order in which to change them. Process and system analysis, a must-do in any organizational change, should be carried out in the design phase of the change process.

This type of analysis is relevant to the following systems, among others: selection, compensation, recognition, information management, career development, job rotation, and promotions. The remainder of this chapter explores each of these systems.

Selection

An organization can move in the proper strategic direction more easily when it hires people who have the skills, ability, and motivation to work in the new culture and achieve the business strategies. Selection, therefore, is one of the most important systems to align; if unaligned, it can negatively affect turnover, productivity, and morale.

It's a given that leaders most commonly identify people as their organization's prime asset. Some even think of employees as fellow explorers on the voyage of change. But, most leaders realize they can't take just anyone along. After they've invested so much to build a value-driven culture, they want to introduce the best candidates into this carefully nurtured environment.

It's also important to note that current employees will soon notice the "new type" of employee coming on board. These new employees, carefully screened to ensure they naturally demonstrate the behaviors the new values require, will act as models. Selecting people for the new culture—a critical, thorough process—is usually a long-term strategy, unless leadership identifies a significant short-term hiring need.

In starting up a new facility, selection of the entire workforce—based on the requirements of the strategic direction—can have an immediate and dramatic impact. Miller Brewing Company's Trenton plant proved leadership's commitment to creating a different environment for that brewery. Leaders wanted an environment in which people worked in teams and accepted responsibility for many of the tasks typically handled by management.

Because they understood the critical nature of hiring the right people, leaders at Miller used a selection process tailored to the environment they were trying to create. This process focused on candidates' teamwork abilities. Miller selected and trained the new employees based on the culture and supporting values it envisioned. This facility frequently is cited as the best Miller brewery, and one of the finest in the world.

Effective candidate selection is as important for filling positions in established companies as it is for hiring people for a start-up. The authors worked with one manufacturing organization that did not use a structured selection process. As a result, its hiring was predictably *un*predictable; the company never quite knew what kind of performance to expect after it had hired someone. This process vacuum also negatively affected employees when management filled positions from within: No one knew why one candidate was promoted instead of another.

The company decided to take positive action to address these issues. It defined sets of skills and abilities (dimensions/competencies) for open positions, based on needs developed for the newly created strategic focus. The organization then implemented a new selection process that used structured interviews to identify candidates' past experience. The company not only developed the process, it trained people to conduct effective interviews.

The new selection process raised the caliber of new hires and ensured that the dimensions they demonstrated would better match those required to achieve critical success factors. It also affected employee morale in an unanticipated, positive way. Employees believed they were treated fairly in placement and promotion decisions because they clearly understood selection and promotion requirements.

With any organizational change, selection system alignment hinges upon hiring based on the assessment of job candidate skills, ability, and motivation to work within the new environment.

Compensation

Nothing captures people's attention quite like pay. Once an organization aligns the selection system to identify individuals with the greatest likelihood of achieving success, it should strive to ensure that its compensation system rewards behavior and performance that support the strategic focus.

Compensation systems have the power to reinforce desired behaviors and communicate areas of development. For example, rewarding the Sales area for customer retention aligns with a value of Customer Service. Rewarding Manufacturing for quality as well as for quantity aligns with a Quality value. Rewarding support groups, such as Engineering, Purchasing, and Accounting, for building internal partnerships, aligns with a Teamwork value.

Sandvik Steel Company wanted to communicate the importance of people's day-to-day performance in achieving critical success factors and affecting overall company performance. Sandvik chose to link its bonus and gain-sharing systems to performance in achieving its CSFs. The company devised a way for each department to track specific measures that are based on Sandvik's CSFs, and it linked gain sharing to those measures. In its unique way Sandvik rewards employees for how well they meet departmental and organizational goals.

The Auburn, California, division of Coherent, Inc., realized that it needed a new compensation system to align with the new high-performance team culture. After much debate, the division chose and installed a gain-sharing program that measured the performance of each team rather than individual performance. It based performance measurements on objective, statistical data regarding a team's quality, on-time delivery, and productivity. And, it based percentage increases on how well each team did when compared with its performance of the previous six months, not against an arbitrary standard. While the merits of providing extrinsic vs. intrinsic rewards can be debated, the division realized and maintained a sizable jump in productivity when gain sharing was implemented.

These changes to the division's compensation system created effective peer evaluations and pay systems. More importantly, they increased employee involvement, morale, learning, responsibility, and accountability. Customer satisfaction also showed an upturn.

Development Dimensions International bases bonuses for client project delivery teams on two factors—customer satisfaction and profitability. As the system stands, a project team must meet both profit and customer expectations to achieve 100 percent of its bonus. This approach prevents maximizing profit at the expense of customer satisfaction. It also aligns behavior with the company's critical success factors and values, which are based on customer retention. Figure 19 shows how DDI's bonus system works. In the matrix 5 exceeds expectations, 3 meets expectations, and 1 fails to meet expectations.

Gross Margin Rating	1	2	3	4	5
5	60%	90%	125%	140%	150%
4	45%	75%	115%	125%	140%
3	30%	60%	100%	115%	125%
2	0%	30%	60%	75%	90%
1	0%	0%	30%	45%	60%

Customer Satisfaction Rating

Figure 19. DDI's Bonus System

Compensation is a major driver of behavior because people tend to act on issues that affect their pay. In any organization at any time, behavior can be influenced by the compensation system. Therefore, aligning this system to reward the behaviors that will achieve the strategic direction immediately focuses employees on the company's strategic goals.

Recognition

Like compensation, recognition is a powerful reinforcer that can affect future behavior. Awards, recognition letters, and public demonstrations of appreciation should recognize achievement and support behavior that demonstrates organizational values.

Siderca, of Argentina, is a major producer of steel pipes for the oil industry. Siderca actively involves more than one-third of its employees in quality improvement efforts, many as members of continuous improvement teams. Each year the organization holds a major celebration designed to recognize the teams and give them an opportunity to share their successes with colleagues. Without the recognition of these process improvement teams, Siderca believes it would not continue to realize quality and productivity improvements.

One global organization launched the Free Lunch for Internal Partners program, dubbed "FLIP," in which peers recognized internal partners for their service. The idea was to reinforce internal efforts to better serve the company's clients. People identified FLIP candidates by completing a brief situation/task-action-result (STAR) description for them and submitting it to management. The COO then personally awarded the recipient with a luncheon gift certificate. The program was unique because peers alone recognized and rewarded one another. Management performed only two functions: congratulating the recipient and providing the free lunch.

Coaching is a value First Chicago NBD encourages. One area of the bank implemented a semiannual recognition program, the First Awards, in which managers and individual contributors (technical experts) are nominated and then selected to receive coaching awards on a semiannual basis. Winners receive public recognition during "All Hands" staff meetings. The bank believes that this ongoing spotlight on coaching helps to instill it as an embedded value at First Chicago NBD.

Rewards programs abound in organizations. Many are relatively simple activity- or objective-based programs. But no matter how simple, the recognition system that focuses on living the values and links the behaviors that support those values helps drive a culture-change strategy.

Information Management

Leaders would do well to ask questions like, "Do employees have the information they need to perform effectively?" Or, if business objectives involve building customer loyalty or using self-managed work groups, the question might be, "Does our information management system provide the right information?" Internal and external customer satisfaction data, production data, and financial data must be more complete than the type of data most information systems currently collect.

A large, national snack-food company relies heavily on employees' knowledge of its business to help them fully contribute toward improving performance. The company trains 8,000 employees throughout 40 manufacturing plants in general business principles and in the specific economics of plant operations. Each work team receives a weekly results scorecard that indicates how it performed against key cost, quality, and service targets. This scorecard graphically highlights easy-to-read information to help the team track its progress during the course of the week. The structure of the data reflects the team's needs rather than the needs of the accounting department. Work teams in this organization use knowledge of their organization's business, combined with this timely, relevant scorecard information, to take action for improving results.

The Customer Service Center at Telstra, a major telecommunications firm in Australia, implemented a "Happy to Help" initiative that focused on improving service levels. Telstra provided extensive training at all levels and aligned many of its systems to support the initiative. The company followed up with new measures of customer service to help representatives track their performance and also posted weekly results and trends in the Customer Service Center.

Customer representatives throughout Blue Cross and Blue Shield of Montana have experienced sweeping changes in processes and systems. Because of the change implementation in the area led by Sherry Cladouhos, vice president of Beneficiary Services, reps in Beneficiary Services can now meet any customer need without handing off work to other areas. Cross-functional teams designed a new method for helping customers get the information they need without being bounced from phone to phone. Each representative's workstation can call up multiple screens for handling customer issues, answering questions, or entering information. Representatives can instantly update information or solve a problem, instead of having to send the problem to another area, losing time and possibly even paperwork.

These examples illustrate the importance of providing the workforce with necessary data on key measurements. Such information is as important to a customer service rep as lunar coordinates were to an Apollo astronaut. Without access to such data, people simply can't perform at a level acceptable to themselves or the organization.

Other Important Systems

The case for aligning organizational systems with the strategic focus is a strong one. The price of misalignment is high. Aside from the systems already discussed, here are some others that should be addressed:

Career development. Career paths no longer follow the traditional hierarchical ladder. Rather, they consist of a broader base of skill development designed to benefit the individual as well as the organization. In a time when loyalty and long-term commitment between company and employee are more difficult, a well-thought-out and aligned career development system can meet business as well as individual needs.

Job rotation. If an organization embeds teamwork and flexibility in its values and structures work around processes, its workforce must be equipped with a variety of skills to be able to work together while having the capability of rotating among several jobs. For some, job rotation also fuels high job satisfaction by adding diversity and challenge to the workday.

Promotions. Few actions kill credibility faster than when an organization talks about the importance of modeling certain positive behaviors, then promotes someone who models the opposite behaviors. In order to achieve a culture-change strategy, promotions should be based on achieving results while supporting values. The people who get promotions are the people who work, interact, and lead in a manner that reinforces the values.

The Continuous Nature of Process and Systems Alignment

Aligning organizational systems with critical success factors and values is an ongoing process. Alignment is also one of the strongest and most effective communication strategies. As people gain more experience and proceed with the organization's change, the need to exercise their talents and potential will naturally lead them to examine more systems. For example, early in the change, people might find it impossible to move from a requirement of four levels of approval down to two. Later on, with the alignment of systems, one approval might become the obvious answer. In another instance it might initially seem threatening to involve peers in the performance feedback process. Later, this can become standard practice.

These benefits, reaped along the way, demonstrate the energy that a value-driven change generates. They serve as a benchmark, confirming that an organization is maintaining the proper course toward a successful implementation.

CHAPTER 11

DESIGN AND IMPLEMENTATION
THROUGH HIGH INVOLVEMENT

U nderstanding the four thrusts lays the foundation for designing and implementing the change effort. During the second and third phases of the value-driven change process, the organization develops a practical plan for making the vision a reality. Work in phase one formulated the strategic focus and used the power of the four thrusts to communicate and activate change. Now, during the design and implementation phases, the four thrusts become the tools for working through many of the issues that are central to the strategic focus. Here the scope and pace of the change are determined, and the change effort is continually monitored and fine-tuned.

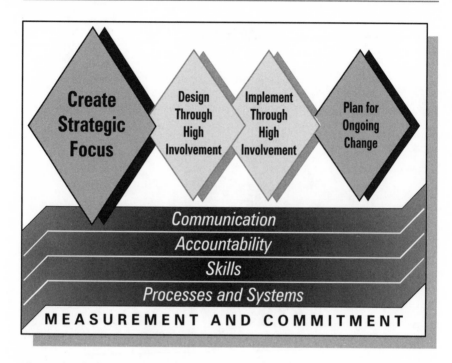

Figure 20. Value-Driven Change Model: Design and Implementation

The Scope of the Change Effort

The toughest decision facing leaders in a culture change is not "Should we do it?" Market or environmental conditions force these changes and render such questions moot. A more difficult and challenging question is "What is the scope of our culture change?" *Scope* takes into account the target areas of change, that is, whether that change involves a department, a division, a geographical location, or the entire company. Scope also takes into account the magnitude of organizational change that the workforce must handle—*How different will the organization be?* and *How many things will need to be done to achieve the vision?*

In determining the scope of a change effort, an organization might wrestle with the concept of reaching a comfortable level of employee involvement. Along the way leaders will face important decisions in several critical areas that affect the short- and long-term courses of their journey. These decisions determine the extent of the change within the organization.

To better handle these critical decisions regarding the scope of the value-driven change, senior leaders can answer a series of questions that will prompt them to address areas of concern in ways that are most appropriate to their particular organization. This approach helps determine the appropriate level of involvement up front and saves time, money, and resources. These questions are:

- *Which areas of the organization will be affected or involved?* Senior leaders at NIBCO tested a high-involvement strategy by implementing an experimental "pilot cell" that streamlined the manufacturing process. This enabled associates in a certain area to cross-train in all jobs that involved moving the product from raw material to finished goods. After achieving measurable success NIBCO instituted a high-performance work system throughout its new Charlestown facility.

- *How different is the vision of tomorrow from the reality of today?* Answering this question means bridging the gap between the present and the future. Leaders can determine the magnitude of the gap by examining the results of self-assessments and surveys conducted during the strategic focus phase of the change effort. At this point leaders will probably realize that changing from a bureaucratic organization—where people stay within the constraints of their own job or department and don't even answer another person's phone—to a proactive service organization will require bridging a considerable gap. The transformation from a revenue-driven organization to one dedicated to customer needs offers a similar challenge in scope.

- *What amount of information will be shared, and with whom?* Many organizations choose to share financial information with employees. More commonly, organizations that encourage employee involvement provide some form of general business training and share measures that not only gauge performance but also reveal how the organization is doing in its particular industry.

Springfield Remanufacturing Corp. (SRC) President Jack Stack is considered to be the pioneer of "open-book management," or the sharing of business and financial information with all employees. In *The Great Game of Business* (1992) Stack chronicled how the open-book management method led to SRC's amazing growth. The book details the impact of information sharing within a company that Stack himself described as "comatose" at its lowest point.

Stack's open-book method involved the companywide distribution of income statements and budget figures. Managers learned how to read financial numbers and passed this knowledge on to employees. The entire company began following financial statements weekly and monthly. Employees benefited from a stock owner-ship plan. Every financial goal that was developed tied into the balance sheet—and so did employee bonuses. Sales began to grow 40 percent a year. SRC stock shot up in value from a low of 10 cents a share to a high of more than 18 dollars. Under Stack's imaginative leadership, information sharing led SRC out of a coma and into prosperity in 10 short years.

- *What amount of decision-making authority will be delegated?* One auto manufacturer authorized customer service representatives to solve customer problems in amounts up to $7,000, while another automaker used a limit of only $1,200. The Shangri-La Hotel in Asia autho-rizes employees to spend up to $500, without approval, to satisfy customers. Part of the decision-making process involving the scope of the organizational change effort involves asking whether supervisors should retain these responsibilities, share them by seeking input from subordinates, or pass them on to individuals or teams.

- *How extensive should training be, and who should receive it?* A company might have to train all its managers, all its sales reps—everyone in the organi-zation. People have a greater chance of succeeding with proper training, which serves two critical purposes in an organization undergoing value-driven change: It develops skills so people can perform better in the new culture, and it communicates clear expectations of how people are to behave in the future.

- *What will reward systems, such as compensation, promotion, and recognition, look like in the revamped organization?* Some organizations reserve bonuses for senior-level leaders only. Others extend eligibility to the far reaches of the organizational structure. In all cases rewards should help shape and drive behavior in the desired direction. Promotions, bonuses, and other rewards send a strong message about what's really important to senior leaders. This message will either reinforce the values that leaders espouse or spotlight hypocrisy.

Proceeding gradually with key issues such as the six above might make the change more palatable, but leaders still have to address these issues to determine the scope of the organization's change. For example, one company might decide that supervisors or production foremen in its manufacturing division will continue to make key operational decisions. Another organization might extend the level of employee involvement to, perhaps, an assembly line worker shutting down the line to correct a defect, even though the cost of that stoppage could rise to $100,000 for 15 minutes of downtime. Some might deem this an inappropriate level of involvement. On the other hand, because that worker is closest to the job, his or her quick fix could head off more serious consequences, perhaps a more extensive shutdown later on.

Within organizations like Miller Brewing, employee teams make decisions about hiring, day-to-day work, and vacation schedules. Their level of involvement, obviously appropriate for the people and the situation, has contributed to the success of Miller's organizational change.

The Pace of the Change Effort

The question "At what pace do we change?" involves a separate but equally difficult set of decisions that leaders must make. Pace involves the length of time needed to achieve the change, taking into account its scope. An organization requires less time to implement a value-driven change when it readily provides information and employs a workforce that has the capabilities and willingness necessary to undertake the change effort. Change in less-equipped organizations takes longer.

Leaders might want to think about the following questions in preparation for determining an appropriate pace for a change effort:

- *Given the scope, how fast can we go?* A change within one department might be accomplished in four months. A change involving the people and processes in a company with 28,000 employees on three continents might require four years. The potentially grave ramifications within the marketplace of waiting four years for full implementation must be considered as well.

- *Can different parts of the organization change at different rates?* It might be impossible for all parts of an organization to change at the same pace. Communication eases the strain when departments or divisions experience change at different times. Making sure people understand the rationale for a particular implementation process avoids certain chaos. Interdepartmental communication must also increase. As an example, a newly empowered marketing team within a large manufacturer of electrodes decided to alter its marketing strategy without involving the sales, manufacturing, or engineering departments. The marketing team, however, quickly realized that empowerment did not negate the importance of communication and teamwork. The team could not effectively implement the new strategy without the knowledge and cooperation of the other departments.

- *Should we modify the scope to quicken the pace?* If the overriding need is speed of implementation, then some elements of scope should be reduced or resequenced to accommodate an accelerated pace. If the overriding need is to broadly change processes and systems, then leaders must allow time for this to happen and realize that it does take time. The organization's needs can create a series of trade-offs—a reality check for leaders seeking change.

Once an organization answers these tough but critical scope and pace questions, it can identify concrete actions to take within the four thrusts of a culture change. With systems aligned and the change effort lifting off the launch pad, the company moves beyond the initial pull of resistance and heads toward its destination.

Participation in the Change Effort Implementation

Once the role of the four thrusts in the change effort is understood, an organization can begin to think about how to involve employees in the design—as it relates to the four thrusts—and in the implementation. For leadership, involvement means communicating information about the status of the organization in transition—its successes and problems. It also means making sure employees directly execute various aspects of the change. This approach addresses both the current and desired cultures. The idea is to foster the notion that "We're all in this together. We can sink or swim, but we'll do it together."

For Blue Cross and Blue Shield of Montana, one of the first steps in the involvement strategy was a meeting of senior leaders to examine the ramifications of such a change and to crystallize their role in the new culture. Jane DeLong remembers: "I facilitated for four hours, and what we came out with at the end of those four hours was a paragraph on leadership, a new definition of leadership. It was really interesting that it took four hours for them to come up with one paragraph that said basic things that are pretty well accepted now in the industry." At that time she recalls, "We had tons of discussions and tons of skepticism because they could feel the pull, the change, and 'Are we really going to be able to pull this off?' and 'Sometimes these efforts aren't always successful.'"

Some common approaches to successful change implementations include:

- Creating a steering committee to manage and drive the change effort.
- Involving the workforce in creating, fine-tuning, and finalizing the strategic focus of the change implementation.

- Chartering cross-functional teams to design and implement changes and monitor improvements in major processes and systems.

- Creating a communication team charged with ongoing implementation of an agreed-to communication strategy.

- Developing other task forces to work on shorter-term projects or actions that did not require ongoing monitoring.

At this critical launch point in the change process, discussing each of these actions will define the nuts and bolts of a successful value-driven change strategy.

The Steering Committee

A steering committee, advisory board, or executive team gives the kind of attention to the change effort that assures its success, whether that change involves high-performance work systems, reengineering, quality, customer focus, or establishment of a competency-based organization. A cross-functional steering team manages the change effort because major change involves high degrees of interdependence across critical functional areas. Too often, one senior line manager—frequently the vice president of human resources—is expected to assume sole responsibility for overseeing a change effort. The most competent executive can't go it alone at this stage. It takes a number of senior leaders, each of whom brings individual abilities to the table, to form a strong aggregate of organizational talent.

This cross-functional steering committee moves to accomplish several significant objectives. It defines the strategic focus; determines the scope and pace of change; involves stakeholders from the organization's key functions in order to minimize vested interests and maximize collaboration; and creates a level of involvement, commitment, and ownership across a broad section of the organization that an individual, even the CEO, can't achieve alone.

Leaders of organizations that are considering change frequently wonder whether one steering committee should handle the entire change effort, or whether steering teams representing each major component of the business—or major geographical location—should share the responsibility. There is no universal answer to this question. In general, one steering committee comprising members from across major business groups usually has the synergy to be most influential. Once again, the concept of *uniqueness* comes into play. Leaders need to decide which steering committee configuration will work best in their organization's business situation and climate.

In one global organization the leadership set up separate steering teams for the Far East, North America, and Europe because each of these operations faced the challenge of addressing a unique set of market issues. This organization's operating committee insisted that the corporate vision and values remain consistent across markets while maintaining a belief that critical success factors could be unique to each area—as long as the CSFs supported the overall corporate vision of customer focus.

To establish an overall direction for Buick's customer focus initiative, leaders at Buick Motor Division formed a customer-loyalty advisory board of 12 members culled from the home office, zone organization, and dealerships. Based on Buick's vision of *Customer Care That Says You're Family*, the board identified four key business objectives (critical success factors) and a set of values that would drive their vision. Members also identified existing processes and systems that were not aligned. Their plan was to modify them to work toward a common direction. Once the advisory board defined Buick's key objectives and values, they undertook a three-year change effort that included actions such as communicating the overall vision to each of the 10 home-office departments, 13 zones, and more than 500 dealerships.

Employee Involvement in Finalizing the Strategic Focus

The launch of a successful value-driven change effort relies first and foremost on a concrete plan that involves the workforce in creating, analyzing, fine-tuning, and finalizing the vision, CSFs, and values. Focus groups, surveys, department discussions, electronic bulletin boards, and town meetings all serve as vehicles for gaining involvement and commitment.

The method best suited to a particular organization depends on the number of employees, their geographical dispersion, and the number of businesses under the organizational umbrella. The underlying philosophy for involving employees at this stage is that they are more likely to work toward achieving a strategic focus that they helped to create.

At Buick once the work of the customer-loyalty advisory board was communicated to the dealership level, each of the dealerships established a six-member steering team comprising the owner or manager and a cross section of sales, technical, and administrative associates. Each steering team defined its unique critical success factors based on individual business needs, but designed them to support the overall Buick vision. Each then created an action plan to meet both dealership and Buick objectives. The process at the dealership level closely paralleled Buick's corporate-level process.

Finally, the customer loyalty initiative was communicated to employees in specific initiative newsletters, dealer presentations, and workshop prework packages. All Buick associates then attended a workshop that provided the information and skills they needed to implement the steering teams' action plans.

By involving associates throughout the organization, from the home office through all dealerships, Buick increased the probability of realizing a successful change implementation. This level of involvement highlighted the importance of designing a sound plan at the advisory board and steering team levels and then following it with aggressive, organizationwide communication of the elements needed for success.

Steering Committee and Cross-Functional Systems Teams

In addition to its other duties, the steering committee establishes either process action teams or system improvement teams to analyze existing systems and recommend changes. This critical function ensures that interdependent processes and systems support the organization's vision and values. Initially, the steering committee takes a "big picture" look at systems and processes to determine those in need of change. Some require fine-tuning. Some need considerable improvement, but not radical change. Others might need a complete overhaul.

The steering committee's review of major organizational systems—compensation, performance management, information management, recognition and reward, and promotion—ensures these systems align with the desired values and behaviors. To repeat an earlier example, a compensation system that provides incentives for volume of sales might encourage different behaviors than one that provides incentives for customer retention.

After completing the alignment review, the steering committee charters system improvement teams and process action teams to examine problem areas and to recommend needed changes. These teams then periodically report progress to the steering committee and seek additional guidance as needed.

Blue Cross and Blue Shield of Montana proceeded with this type of team through what they call *changemaker teams*. "The changemaker teams are all very enthusiastic about their mission," says Vice President Jane DeLong. "They're involved with supporting the entire culture in various ways. The training changemaker team is working to make our training consistent throughout the company. The performance management change-maker team is working to change the performance management system to a more participative process, focusing on the corporate vision and values."

System improvement teams and process action teams typify how involvement can facilitate culture change. They move the transition along largely by aligning systems in support of the new culture and the strategic focus.

Mandatory Communication Team

As stated early on, change efforts fail often—50 to 80 percent of the time. In the wake of such resounding defeats, senior leaders allude to an organizational culture that didn't support the business strategy. According to T.J. and Sandar Larkin in their 1996 *Harvard Business Review* article, "In 1993, Wyatt Company (now Watson Wyatt Worldwide) investigated 531 U.S. organizations undergoing major restructuring. Wyatt asked the CEOs, 'If you could go back and change one thing, what would it be?' The most frequent answer: The way I communicated with my employees" (p. 95).

Given this scenario, all organizations undergoing a change effort should establish a communication team that includes leaders and, more importantly, nonleaders who will increase commitment and generate creative ways to support the values and the change initia-tive. The communication team, usually a permanent one, conveys the objectives and progress of the change effort to people throughout the organization. It generates support to help solidify behaviors that demonstrate organizational values. And it presents ideas to senior leaders for using formal communication vehicles in a way that is most appropriate for the organization and the situation.

Some large companies already have in place communications or public relations departments. During a change effort the imposing size of these departments can cause employees to feel disconnected from such groups. On the other hand, a communication team created by the steering committee helps to involve others within the organization: first to give a fresh perspective of the current communication system, then to use it to support the new culture.

Mandatory communication teams bring with them many benefits, but there's one danger. A change effort that includes a communication team but lacks training for that team becomes an advertising campaign. Without training in the role of communication during a change effort, the team will do what it has seen done before—create ads that use buttons, T-shirts, or balloons. This team needs to understand that the purpose of communication is to make progress visible, not to preach the message. Preaching creates a credibility gap because it leaves the workforce unclear about the purpose of the effort.

Task Forces

The steering committee can charter a task force to handle a short-term project related to the change. A task force, responsible for a specific job, disbands after its work is done because the specific task is closed ended and requires no monitoring. The task force level of a major change effort involves pulling in a cross section of employees from the entire organization. This level of involvement can generate the degree of commitment that overcomes barriers to change.

Stages of the Change Effort

In any organizational change employee reaction to new processes, systems alignment, and human resource policies will follow predictable patterns. If leaders understand these patterns, they can take action to reduce the stress that employees will experience during the change. Such stress is heartfelt and intensely personal because organizational change affects the place where people earn their living and spend most of their waking hours.

As intense and personal as workforce reaction can be, it still tends to fall into four distinct stages, which follow. Leaders who become familiar with the nature of these stages can better manage a change effort.

Stage 1: Awareness

If an imminent change is properly communicated, people will be well aware of it. If the communication system fails to operate effectively, organizational change can seem to explode onto the scene. In either case awareness marks the short period of time (a few seconds or a week) during which people recognize that things aren't—or won't be—the same anymore, that something is changing the way they work, relate to one another, and think about their jobs.

Responses to change cover the spectrum of emotions. Some employees embrace change. Others see only a nightmare. Many are skeptical. Most go along with it and keep their opinions to themselves. The intensity of personal reactions distinguishes this stage from the other three. Here, communication eases the fear of the unknown and prepares people for what is to come. Senior leaders might be concerned that their communications have somehow created these diverse reactions. In reality this is the way any group of employees will react at the onset of change.

Stage 2: Disorientation

After the change has been announced, people begin to see a difference in the workplace and in their jobs. Often they find that one change triggers several others, and what initially seemed to be simple becomes a complex chain reaction. Perhaps a new process solves an old problem—but creates several new ones.

Meanwhile, everyone continues to face the stress of deadlines, meetings, quotas, customer needs, and so on. They might wonder if anyone is really in charge, or what the priorities are or should be, or what is expected of them in addition to what they already face. More than anything, employees learn in this stage that change, even welcome change, can be disorienting. People who embraced the change might lose their confidence and enthusiasm, while those who opposed it believe their greatest fears are coming true.

This is the figurative adolescence of the change effort, when behaviors can be unpredictable and sometimes alarming. Leaders should continually remind themselves that once this storm is weathered, better times are ahead.

Stage 3: Reorientation

With changes in place, the workforce begins to reestablish a sense of personal control. Fear of the unknown becomes comfort with the known. Work in a common direction begins to pay off. Some tension remains, but people are less concerned about it because they feel more confident of their abilities. In fact, they might feel as if they've done enough to adjust to the changes and incorporate them in their lives. They might resist doing more, even though the change has not yet been fully integrated.

At this point employees face the danger of overconfidence, which might lead to a premature end of monitoring the change. In addition, overconfidence leads to lack of focus to the task at hand, which can result in a stumbling effort and lack of results.

Stage 4: Integration

In this stage employee integration and acceptance of the change make it habit. Here, people say, "That's the way we do things around here." When change is integrated, it isn't considered extra work. It is embedded in everyone's daily routine.

Employees vaguely recall how they used to do things, and they can't quite imagine doing it that way now. Questions about the change are no longer asked. Instead, people scrutinize new challenges and areas in need of improvement. They possess a thorough knowledge of realigned systems and processes, which they are quick to share with vendors and customers.

Managing Change

There can be no doubt that the implementation of change causes disruption. Part of overseeing change involves managing this disruption by handling resistance and by helping people deal with changes to the routine and general disorientation. Leaders who understand these ramifications soon understand the need for constant communication during the change effort.

An organization moving from the initiation stage into disorientation might feel as if it's a rocket hitting the upper atmosphere. Resistance and external pressures can cause superheating. People grow weary of the strain. Then comes reorientation and the resulting relief that disorientation is at an end, and everyone can get back to business as usual.

As one change leads to another, particularly in a major change effort involving several years, the four phases of change serve as a reminder of the condition of the workforce. The introduction of each revamped system or process begins a new cycle of disorientation and reorientation, which become part of the fabric of the ongoing organizational change.

CHAPTER 12

A PLAN FOR ONGOING CHANGE: KEEPING CHANGE ALIVE

☆ ☆ ☆

The vision of exploring new frontiers did not end when U.S. astronauts landed on the moon. The lunar landing was only part of a natural progression that began when Project Mercury launched an American out of earth's atmosphere. Project Gemini added two more requirements for a lunar landing—space walks and the docking of two manned space vehicles. The first Apollo mission ended in tragedy with an oxygen fire during a countdown exercise, a horrible misstep that cost the lives for three astronauts. Still, the vision remained in place, and the effort continued.

NASA's subsequent Apollo missions orbited the moon and tested the docking of the command and lunar modules. Then came Apollo 11's success, which was repeated several times with the notable exception of Apollo 13. A later Apollo mission featured docking with the Soviet Soyuz space station—an event that would have been unthinkable during the time of Sputnik and Yuri

Gagarin. Project Apollo ended and was replaced by the space shuttle, a reusable reentry vehicle. Concurrently, satellites began exploring the remote frontiers of our solar system.

For more than three decades, the space program that began with John F. Kennedy's vision escalated its expectations in the exploration of space. It has established new benchmarks and set new goals that still align with that vision. Where once the objective was to walk on the moon, man now envisions living in outer space. Discussions of manned voyages to Mars have become as common-place as close-up photos of the Martian terrain.

The Ongoing Process

Organizations in business and cultural transition similarly experience the achievements associated with new strategies while overcoming adversities. Far from the end, this phase of ongoing change actually marks the beginning of an improved, aligned, finely tuned organization.

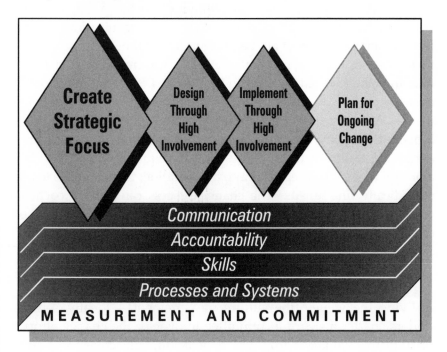

Figure 21. Value-Driven Change Model: Plan for Ongoing Change

In the fourth phase of the value-driven change process, Plan for Ongoing Change, the people responsible for the transition (typically senior leaders) take the changes that have become an integral part of business life and build on them with further improvement in mind. It's not until this point that movement toward the new vision becomes perpetual, and that the organization and all the people in it see and feel the real impact of change.

As discussed in the previous chapter, initiating a particular change or group of changes is followed by disorientation and reorientation. New changes roll in like waves onto a beach, and the process of disorientation and reorientation repeats itself. Keeping change alive down the road, in the reorientation and integration stages, involves continually elevating expectations. The change thrives in such an environment, and monitoring, measuring, and fine-tuning key elements of the organization assure that both the business and culture remain vital.

Ongoing Monitoring and Measurement

Organizations that truly understand the power of a shared set of values in driving change must also realize that organizations rarely live all their values or hit all their targets all the time. It's important to remember, once again, that organizations are populated with human beings, so setbacks are to be expected. A company should no more anticipate hitting all its marks than it should expect to install a new piece of equipment in a manufacturing facility and see it operate in sync with every other piece of equipment in the operation. Typically, even the highest quality equipment needs to be adjusted when it is integrated into an operation; then, it needs to be periodically fine-tuned. The change process can be approached with the same mind-set—continual monitoring by everyone in the organization, particularly the steering committee, helps to keep the change effort on track.

Any discussion of the organizational change process includes, as recurring themes, the importance of having change targets and of living the values (the culture measurement). Ideally, senior leaders charter a steering committee to oversee the change effort. That team evaluates progress in achieving objectives that are designed to realize the organization's vision, achieve its critical success factors, and live its values. For continued success the team does this on a regular basis in a variety of ways, some of which will be discussed later.

Monitoring the culture includes methods such as internal values surveys and customer feedback surveys, both of which build continuous improvement into the value-driven change process. These surveys generate new opportunities for improvement, which in turn generate action to support a culture change and move it forward.

Raising Expectations—Continually

On day one of the change, *doing things a new way* in the eyes of employees might mean answering the phone with a different greeting. A couple of years later, change can mean moving from functional departments to product-centered teams or units, installing new computer systems, or expanding into a foreign market. The waves of change keep lapping at the beach, creeping higher with each pass so that after two years, few stop to think just how significant those changes have been.

After two years, however, senior leaders must continue to be vigilant about fine-tuning. They should continually use monitoring data to modify alignment actions within appropriate change thrusts or to identify any other actions that might be required to remove barriers and facilitate progress.

The steering committee should also fine-tune the effort by moving responsibility for action to a greater number of people who serve as leaders in any function and at any particular time within the organization. For example, each business would structure its annual business plan around the organization's CSFs, strategies, and values. If any single business unit strategy fails to link with the organization's strategic focus, the unit's business plan most likely will not contribute to overall success. In this case leaders would delete this strategy from the business plan.

This is not to say that adjustments should be made only when measurement shows a deficiency. When the implemented changes have become a way of life, senior leaders should raise expectations to keep the change effort from stagnating—even when all measurements appear to be positive.

This phase also provides other opportunities for adjustment. In the initial phases of the change process, organizations might resist the temptation to undertake all the activities required to align every system or process. The ongoing change part of the process provides a chance to review alignment opportunities developed in the strategic focus, identify additional actions that will accelerate progress, and fine-tune accordingly.

Keeping Change Alive

Many organizations model the tremendous possibilities inherent in this stage of the value-driven change process. Leaders at Mott's USA recently undertook an extensive analysis of their change effort. The steering team conducted a broad-based internal survey to look at their new performance management system and also Mott's vision, values, and critical success factors.

The analysis led to a number of adjustments. The steering team members reviewed the corporate vision and made modifications. They revisited the values to more precisely redefine them so that each value better meshed with the performance management system. The team established additional measurements for the critical success factors, which had been difficult to analyze. They also made necessary adjustments to the performance management system in response to employee feedback. Mott's serves as a text-book example of raising expectations to achieve the vision and move successfully into the future.

The change effort at LaRoche Industries began with the need to create a high-performance culture across all business units and manufacturing facilities. This need dictated a redesign of work processes. For this change effort LaRoche chose to implement a team-based design. By the third year of change, leaders within the company were working to firm up their new way of doing things to make it a part of their culture and the norm for conducting busi-ness. Their work centered on three areas:

1. Establishing and solidifying role clarity so that people understood their roles and responsibilities in the new environment.

2. Renewing their commitment to continuous learning through ongoing education and development of all employees.

3. Implementing new selection and performance management systems in support of the team-based design.

Leaders and teams at LaRoche Industries have been able to establish new norms in the company's culture strategy, achieving widespread change in the way employees accomplish their work and in how they work with one another. LaRoche expects similar results throughout the organization, as leaders and teams continue to implement and refine their new way of doing business.

Buick Motor Division maintained a successful, ongoing change by continuing the work of its culture-change initiative to build customer loyalty. The primary action Buick took was to keep its customer loyalty advisory board (dealers, field representatives, and the senior leaders who initiated the change effort) intact for more than three years.

The responsibilities of this board included monitoring the measures established in the strategic focus, recommending course corrections, and proposing follow-up actions to keep the effort moving. This process included additional training and sharing best practices with dealership personnel, particularly in the areas of leading change and managing quality improvement. The board also continually reviewed processes and systems that needed to be aligned with the objective of building customer loyalty.

Other actions within Buick that supported ongoing change included:

- Training Buick managers in the 360° multirater feedback process and providing subsequent coaching to ensure management's success in the new culture.

- Modifying the managers' bonus plan to encourage and recognize their role and support in driving the culture change.

- Using corporatewide communication vehicles to continually support the change effort among employees and dealers.

Buick's dealership steering teams also provided ongoing support following the initial implementation. They attended one-day follow-up sessions to select and charter problem-solving teams, establish strategic teams to ensure long-term success, and familiarize new employees with the customer loyalty initiative.

Into the Future

Throughout the value-driven change process, the commitment, patience, and perseverance of senior leaders determine the level of organizational success. This is true in all stages of planning and implementation, but particularly when change has become a way of life, and excellence means new objectives and new benchmarks.

At this point a leader tends to look ahead to the next challenge. No one is likely to tap that leader on the shoulder and ask, "Have you considered how your people feel about the change? Have you taken a look at your measures lately? What is the current state of the change effort?" In reality, however, this is the time when success really begins, making it the most important phase of the process.

Ironically, this is also the time when leaders' attention might stray—now that they perceive the company as running more smoothly. It seems a lifetime since the organization received the wake-up call for change—a lifetime of challenge and accomplishment. But having come so far, leaders must find the self-discipline and extra effort to ensure that the change process continues. Monitoring, measuring, and continually raising expectations for excellence will help them do this.

Many organizations reach the crossroads of change, and leaders know that choosing the wrong path at this dangerous intersection can mean disaster. When facing major challenges, effective leaders choose to embrace change and set their sights on the vision of a better tomorrow.

The commitment to take the path of organizational change is not to be made lightly. Senior leaders who take this step accept a responsibility that will remain theirs for the life of the company. There is no going back. There is no stopping. There is only the dedication of those leaders to continually seek a new and better, carefully chosen path toward outstanding performance and bottom-line success for the organization.

Your Critical Role in Organizational Change

An Open Letter to Senior Leaders

from Robert W. Rogers,
Chief Operating Officer, DDI

This book frequently discusses the critical role of senior leaders in a culture change initiative. Usually we communicate this criticality in one-on-one conversations with leaders. Hopefully, this message, for now, will be a viable substitute for such a conversation.

In my experience managing change in various organizations, including DDI (where we've applied many of the ideas in this book), I discovered that the key determining factor in the success or failure of change is a leader's ability to become an *articulate advocate* for the change effort.

This belief in a leader's powerful influence goes back to my days as an officer in the U.S. Air Force. One of the most impressive generals I worked with hammered home the point that we must become, and always remain, articulate advocates of air power. This advocacy meant demonstrating a passion for air power—constantly and enthusiastically communicating its positive use. Culture-change efforts require this same type of passion, and as leaders, the role of articulate advocate is ours. Some leaders feel uncomfortable taking on this critical role. But, if we do not accept such responsibility, the change effort has little chance of success.

Part of this responsibility involves doing things that aren't appealing. Frankly, I was once uncomfortable with directly addressing conflict, providing behavioral feedback to another senior executive, making a difficult decision about an employee, or advocating a new policy or procedure with enthusiasm or passion—for the twentieth time. For me, these were all acquired skills. In effect, I had to accept the responsibility of articulating the change.

Existing literature on change refers to the leader's role as a *champion of change*. I prefer the term *articulate advocate*. Personally, it's easier for me to demonstrate the behaviors if I think of the role in this way. There are two key aspects of the articulate advocate role: developing a passion for the change and then demonstrating that passion.

Senior leaders must spearhead a major change effort with passion as well as with logic and rationale. We cannot only believe in our *heads* that the change is right; we must feel it in our *hearts* as well. If you can't feel that the change is right, don't make it—leave things alone. If you don't feel the passion, you can't be the articulate advocate your organization will desperately need. You won't stay the course in the face of the resistance and objections you're bound to experience. You won't possess the resolve needed to counter the politics of people who believe they'll lose out in the change effort. The power to over-come major turf issues doesn't lie within the logical framework of analysis but within your passion to make things better. The combination of logic and passion—your head and your heart— gets the right things done, and done well.

How do you demonstrate the passion? You must constantly be out there communicating the positive and explaining the need for change. There's no such thing as *overcommunicating*. In my experience you need to be eyeball-to-eyeball with people, so everyone can see your passion and commitment. You need to talk almost all the time—at staff meetings as well as company parties and picnics—in fact, everywhere you go. Ask questions, get reactions, listen, ask more questions—and then cajole, beg, and advocate. And when you think you've done enough, start all over again because you'll find that with all you've done—all the talking, cajoling, and advocating—*you haven't done enough*. This out-front advocacy doesn't require a leader with charisma— it just takes commitment, sincerity, and hard work.

It's important to be comfortable in your advocacy, so take care to find activities that suit you best. I'd like to share some articulate advocate actions I've taken that suit my personality. At DDI I have:

- Published the results of my own performance review in the company newsletter. My results objectives reflect the company's critical success factors—including overall profit.

- Asked about customer satisfaction and employee development during casual conversations, rather than focusing on revenue.

- Actively headed DDI's Quality Steering Committee and our Diversity Task Force.

- Led half-day sessions to help people understand the values and how to live them.

- Conducted customer scorecards to support the value of Customer Satisfaction.

- Discouraged cost-reduction strategies that would lead to having inconvenient travel schedules, traveling three consecutive weeks to deliver training, or lodging in unsafe areas—all in support of our Quality of Life for Associates value.

- Eliminated bonuses that encourage our sales associates to pursue new customers rather than service current clients.

- Discharged employees who exceeded their financial goals but could not live our values even after repeated feedback (a regrettable but necessary action).

Success stories about organizational change always include an articulate advocate at the top. The value-driven change process in this book serves as a great blueprint for organizational change; but, without commitment, passion, and effort, all we have is ink on paper. You are the builder—the driving force—for that change. I wish you the best of luck in your quest for change that works.

Bob Rogers

Appendix A

Value-Driven Change Process Applications

Many valuable initiatives or technology applications intended to improve organizational performance rely on the support of the culture within the organization. A business in transition must be able to explain how it will contribute to the strategic focus, how the new values will support success, and which systems will be aligned in the change effort. To ensure success in a change effort, the value-driven change process includes methods for accomplishing all of these.

Applications of the process could include:

- Creating competency-based organizations.
- Designing high-performance work systems.
- Transforming the human resource function.
- Implementing mergers and acquisitions.
- Creating high-involvement organizations.
- Creating a service culture.
- Reengineering.

Leaders often ask if they can implement the value-driven change process while working on other change initiatives. They also wonder if they can apply the process to different types of change efforts. The answer to both questions is yes. And it's easier than one might think, because the process focuses on the human side. Whether an organization is contemplating a process change, new technology, or a new business strategy, its success depends on people behaving differently. Because the value-driven change process emphasizes behavioral change, it is an excellent map for any change effort in which people make the difference between success and failure. This section provides insights and examples of how the process works with other change efforts.

Application: Reengineering

Smaller groups, such as task forces and steering committees, usually design the plan for a reengineering effort. Implementation, however, involves many people. Seventy percent of reengineering efforts fail because the commitment and buy-in of the design team do not transfer to the people involved in the implementation. The value-driven change process improves the odds for success because it increases involvement and buy-in and translates the abstract concepts of change into specific actions that support the reengineering effort.

Example

A large European bank used the value-driven change process to reengineer its entire branch banking operation. Implementation plans included securing senior leaders' buy-in, developing supporting communication strategies, identifying required new skills at all levels, and selecting people for the redesigned jobs. Further leadership review of the organization's four thrusts—communication, accountability, skills, and processes and systems—highlighted areas that needed to be aligned with the change. One such area involved unclear accountabilities for segments of the bank's communication plan. In response, the bank established responsibility for measurement systems and made sure to clearly delineate responsibilities for managing the change at each leadership level.

Application: Mergers and Acquisitions

It can take years to fully integrate two organizations after a merger or acquisition. Most companies focus on blending operations but typically give little attention to blending cultures. In this case the value-driven change process serves as a plan for designing one strong culture from two seemingly competitive ones. A clear map will provide a renewed sense of direction and reduce the degree of ambiguity that a merger or acquisition can create.

Example

The vice president of sales for a Canadian pharmaceutical company quickly learned that a recent acquisition presented him with two distinct cultures. Sales representatives received mixed messages from sales managers, who didn't understand expectations or which behaviors to reinforce. The vice president, realizing that only decisive action would keep the sales force together, applied the value-driven change process to help sales managers from both organizations develop a common vision, critical success factors, and values. As a result, the newly integrated sales force clearly understood its destination and what was expected of it. Sales managers then reinforced the redesign by building expectations into the performance management system and other supporting systems.

Example

Because of the turmoil and uncertainty following its recent acquisition by another company, a large Canadian bank thought it fruitless to strategically plan its corporate direction and values. Despite this perception several divisions of the acquired bank used the value-driven change process to define their own visions, values, and critical success factors. Within two years these divisions grew in size and market share, while maintaining the unique culture that made the acquisition attractive in the first place. Divisions that did not use a strong change process became extinct.

Application: Start-Ups

Start-ups provide a unique opportunity to build a culture from scratch. The value-driven change process provides an effective map for start-ups in which the vision includes highly involved, committed employees and few layers of management. Critical success factors usually focus on quality of new hires, schedules, facility design, training, and orientation, and the four thrusts support new hires in creating the desired culture and core values.

Example

A large manufacturing company followed the value-driven change process to open a facility in a foreign country. The process model helped the start-up team understand the relationships among job design, job dimensions/competencies, selection, and ongoing performance feedback and their use as tools for creating and maintaining a culture. To fit the desired culture, the company selected people who clearly understood their roles, expectations, and the value of teamwork and collaboration. Their success in meeting initial start-up objectives and continuing to meet quality and production goals provides evidence of the effectiveness of the value-driven change process.

Application: Self-Directed Work Teams

For a variety of excellent business reasons, some companies decide to restructure all or part of the organization around work processes and self-directed teams. Success with such implementations relies on organizational support to ensure that the culture will be appropriate and that human resource systems will be aligned. In addition to systems alignment, the model should be applied again to make sure that a team-based organization will have significant impact on business objectives and that the organization truly values teamwork, customer orientation, and continuous improvement.

Example

A major food distribution center implemented a performance management system that encouraged and supported teams in developing their own goals, tracking performance, and providing individual behavioral feedback. The new system shifted the responsibility and ownership of team and individual performance from management to the teams, increasing people's accountability and involvement.

Application: Health Care

The entire health care industry is implementing major changes to work structure and job design. The purpose of the shift is to improve the continuity of care by limiting the number of people who come in contact with any one patient. These patient-centered initiatives call for multi-skilled caregivers who now need new technical skills and must respond to a new set of behavioral expectations. Using a defined process to manage this major change can create the behavioral expectations necessary for providing advanced patient care.

Example

The University of Cincinnati Medical Center used the value-driven change process to establish guiding principles, or values, for patient-centered care. Each unit then identified practices that would help people live those principles. This design, which was implemented in a relatively short period of time, created continuity throughout the organization while maintaining each unit's identity.

Application: Service Quality

Many organizations have identified the need to establish a customer-focused organization by creating a service quality culture. Their business, rather than being transaction focused, relies on increasing customer loyalty in a very competitive market. The value-driven change process can ensure that the organization has an appropriate vision, along with one or two critical success factors that address customer appreciation. The driving value, customer orientation, then becomes the focal point for aligning systems and processes.

Example

The Buick Motor Division of General Motors, mentioned throughout this book, is an excellent example of value-driven change based on a customer satisfaction initiative.

Application: Micro Change

All change efforts need a clear picture of the end state (vision) and what needs to be accomplished (CSFs) and an explanation of how people need to work together (values). The value-driven change process can guide smaller change initiatives that might require modified support systems, new skills, clear accountability, and proactive communication.

Example

A pharmaceutical company looking at a reengineering effort quickly realized that its sales force constituted a bureaucracy with little decision-making authority. To address this situation, management applied the value-driven change process exclusively to this part of the business rather than to the entire organization. The new sales function then identified its own values, CSFs, and systems alignment initiatives to create a truly focused sales force.

Appendix B

☆ ☆ ☆

Four Thrusts
Development Continuum

Communication

Stage	Transition of Values	Characteristics
1–Traditional	Values focus on profit, sales, and authority.	■ Limited/Few formal communications. ■ Symbols reinforce status/hierarchy. ■ Most senior person dominates meetings.
2–Getting Started	Existing values analyzed.	■ Few formal communications; nonessential topics. ■ Symbols analyzed. ■ Meeting frequency increases; effectiveness does not. ■ Leaders aware of importance of their behavior.
3–Making Progress	New/Revised values articulated but not practiced.	■ Communications share business/financial data. ■ Negative symbols eliminated. ■ Meeting effectiveness analyzed. ■ Leaders occasionally use new behaviors.
4–Accelerating	Any conflict between old and new values resolved.	■ Communications plan in place; information supports involvement. ■ Positive symbols introduced. ■ Meeting process improved. ■ Leaders behave positively, even under stress.
5–Full Speed	Values focus on customer satisfaction.	■ Communications open, frequent, and directed toward people who need it. ■ Symbols reinforce new values. ■ Meetings: effective; called/led by people involved in project/topic; participation balanced. ■ Leaders consistently model new values.

Accountability

Stage	Transition of Values	Characteristics
1–Traditional	Values focus on profit, sales, and authority.	■ Hierarchical, multilayered structure. ■ Narrow job/role design focuses on tasks. ■ Managers/Leaders make decisions, control work. ■ Managers/Leaders set all performance objectives.
2–Getting Started	Existing values analyzed.	■ Organizational structure analyzed. ■ Job/Role design still narrow; some job rotation and enrichment. ■ Teams used only for peripheral functions. ■ Managers/Leaders set most performance objectives.
3–Making Progress	New/Revised values articulated but not practiced.	■ Organizational restructuring begins. ■ Job/Role design analyzed. ■ Design/Implementation of some natural and cross-functional teams. ■ Individuals/New teams help determine objectives and make recommendations on decisions.
4–Accelerating	Any conflict between old and new values resolved.	■ Organizational layers reduced. ■ Job/Role redesign begins. ■ Individuals and natural work teams take on operational responsibility; cross-functional teams form, complete projects, and disband easily. ■ Setting performance objectives shared.
5–Full Speed	Values focus on customer satisfaction.	■ Organizational structure facilitates core processes and focuses on customer. ■ Jobs/Roles and teams designed to encompass entire process/product. ■ Individuals/Teams make and implement decisions. ■ Individuals, teams, functional areas set own objectives to align with vision and values.

Skills

Stage	Transition of Values	Characteristics
1–Traditional	Values focus on profit, sales, and authority.	• Development receives little or no attention. • Interactive and leadership skills ignored. • Competition between functions and departments.
2–Getting Started	Existing values analyzed.	• Skills learned as needed; no training plan. • Interactive and leadership skills introduced to leaders. • Teamwork emphasized but not achieved.
3–Making Progress	New/Revised values articulated but not practiced.	• New values articulated; not practiced consistently. • Training plan developed but not a priority. • People learn about interactive skills. • Internal customers/partners concept introduced.
4–Accelerating	Any conflict between old and new values resolved.	• Individuals, team members, leaders contribute to training plan and cross-train. • Everyone receives value-linked interactive and leadership skills training. • Internal partners and teamwork concepts emphasized and achieved sporadically.
5–Full Speed	Values focus on customer satisfaction.	• Required skills identified and trained systematically; training viewed as investment. • Everyone trained in leadership and interactive skills; leaders are effective coaches; view associates as internal partners. • Functional areas, departments, individuals work as partners.

Processes and Systems

Stage	Transition of Values	Characteristics
1–Traditional	Values focus on profit, sales, and authority.	■ Each process and system viewed as discrete entity. ■ Process improvements are management directed.
2–Getting Started	Existing values analyzed.	■ Conflict among processes, systems, and values analyzed with employee input.
3–Making Progress	New/Revised values articulated but not practiced.	■ Process action teams and system-improvement teams formed. ■ Process and system alignment begins.
4–Accelerating	Any conflict between old and new values resolved.	■ Organizational structures examined for consistency with processes and systems. ■ Some systems aligned; most obvious mixed messages eliminated.
5–Full Speed	Values focus on customer satisfaction.	■ Systems aligned and integrated; change and continuous improvement a way of life. ■ Process improvements employee owned. ■ Systems changed based on employee input. ■ Teams permanently organized around processes.

REFERENCES

Aguayo, R., & Deming, W.E. (1991). *Dr. Deming: The American who taught the Japanese about quality.* New York: Simon & Schuster Trade.

Covey, S.R. (1989). *The 7 habits of highly effective people.* New York: Simon & Schuster, Fireside Books.

Covey, S.R. (1990). *Principle-centered leadership.* New York: Simon & Schuster, Summit Books.

Deming, W.E. (1995). *The new economics for industry, government, and education.* Cambridge: Massachusetts Institute of Technology, Center for Advanced Engineering Study.

Dimmick, K.C. (1992). *Effective peer evaluations and pay systems for self-managed work teams: Lessons learned at Coherent, Inc.* An abstract presented at an International Conference on Self-Managed Work Teams sponsored by the University of North Texas.

Frost, P.J., Moore, L.F., Louis, M.R., Lundberg, C.C., & Martin, J. (1986). *Organizational culture.* Beverly Hills, CA: Sage Publications.

General Electric (1991) *Annual Report.* Welch, J.F., Jr., & Hood, E. E., Jr.

Howard, A., Bechet, T.P., Bray, D.W., Burke, W.W., Byham, W.C., Fisher, K., Lawler, E.E. III, Levinson, H., Nadler, D.A., Rogers, R.W., Walker, J.W., Walton, E., & Zemke, R.E. (1994). *Diagnosis for organizational change: Methods and models.* New York: The Guilford Press.

Joiner, B.L., & Deming, W.E. (1994). *Fourth generation management: The new business consciousness.* New York: McGraw-Hill.

Jones, P., & Kahaner, L. (1995). *Say it and live it: The 50 corporate mission statements that hit the mark.* New York: Doubleday.

Kaplan, R.S., & Norton, D.P. (1992, January–February). The balanced scorecard—Measures that drive performance. *Harvard Business Review,* 71–79.

Kaplan, R.S., & Norton, D.P. (1993, September–October). Putting the balanced scorecard to work. *Harvard Business Review,* 134–137.

Kaplan, R.S., & Norton, D.P. (1996, January–February). Using the balanced scorecard as a strategic management system. *Harvard Business Review,* 75–85.

Kawasaki, G. (1995). *How to drive your competition crazy: Creating disruption for fun and profit.* New York: Hyperion.

Kotter, J. P., & Heskett, J.L. (1992). *Corporate culture and performance.* New York: Simon & Schuster, The Free Press.

Larkin, T.J., & Larkin, S. (1996, May–June). Reaching and changing frontline employees. *Harvard Business Review,* 95–104.

Lawler, E.E. III. (1992). *The ultimate advantage: Creating the high-involvement organization.* San Francisco: Jossey-Bass.

Moskal, B.S. (1996, November 18). CEOs speak out. *IndustryWeek,* 13–18.

Oran, M., & Wellins, R.S. (1995). *Re-engineering's missing ingredient: The human factor.* London: Institute of Personnel and Development.

Ross, D.L., & Benson, J.A. (1995, October). Cultural change in ethical redemption: A corporate case study. *Journal of Business Communication, 32n4,* 345–362.

Schneider, B., Brief, A.P., & Guzzo, R.A. (1996, Spring). Creating a climate and culture for sustainable organizational change. *Organizational Dynamics,* 7–19.

Schuster, J.R., & Zingheim, P.K. (1992). *The new pay: Linking employee and organizational performance.* New York: Simon & Schuster, Lexington Books, The Free Press.

Senge, P.M. (1990). *The fifth discipline: The art and practice of the learning organization.* New York: Doubleday.

Shepard, A., Slayton, D., Barbree, J., & Benedict, H. (1994). *Moon shot: The inside story of America's race to the moon.* Atlanta: Turner Publishing.

Stack, J. (with Burlingham, B.). (1992). *The great game of business.* New York: Doubleday.

Stevens, T. (1996, November 18). Follow the leader. *IndustryWeek,* 16–17.

Stewart, T.A. (1996, September 30). A refreshing change: Vision statements that make sense. *Fortune,* 195–196.

Strebel, P. (1996, May–June). Why do employees resist change? *Harvard Business Review,* 86–92.

The Human Resource Planning Society (HRPS). Presented at the 1996 HRPS Annual Conference, April 1996. *It's deja future all over again: Are you getting ready?* SOTA 96, Round II Report. New York: Ulrich, D., & Eichinger, R.

Topolnicki, D.M. (1996, January). 100 top schools in towns you can afford. *Money Magazine, 25n1,* 108.

Webster, C. (1995). Marketing culture and marketing effectiveness in service firms. *Journal of Services Marketing* [On-line], *9n2,* 6–21. Available: ABI/INFORM 16364.00 Article Ref. No.: B-JSV-34-1.

Wellins, R.S., Byham, W.C., & Dixon, G.R. (1994). *Inside teams: How 20 world-class organizations are winning through teamwork.* San Francisco: Jossey-Bass.

Wellins, R.S., Byham, W.C., & Wilson, J.M. (1991). *Empowered teams: Creating self-directed work groups that improve quality, productivity, and participation.* San Francisco: Jossey-Bass.

Wilson, J.M., George, J., Wellins, R.S., with Byham, W.C. (1994). *Leadership trapeze: Strategies for leadership in team-based organizations.* San Francisco: Jossey-Bass.

Zuboff, S. (1988). *In the age of the smart machine: The future of work and power.* New York: Basic Books.

ABOUT DEVELOPMENT DIMENSIONS INTERNATIONAL

Development Dimensions International (DDI) is an international human resource company that specializes in helping clients improve their business performance by aligning people strategies with business strategies. DDI works in close partnership with clients to assess their organizations and people, develop and implement practical strategies, and achieve measurable improvements in organizational and individual performance.

DDI helps organizations develop an appropriate strategic focus and then align systems and processes that focus on achieving their vision of success. DDI also works with clients to create high-performance cultures in which selection, training and development, and performance management all link and work together. Specific areas of expertise include:

- Managing and implementing change at all levels of the organization.

- Developing a service culture focused on meeting customer needs.

- Executing leadership and workforce development to build management, interpersonal, and team skills at all levels.

- Hiring and promoting world-class people in an efficient, fair, and legally credible manner.

- Outsourcing for assessment, selection, and interpersonal skills training and executive development.

- Selecting and developing workforces for facility start-ups and expansions.

Organized to design and implement customized solutions for each client, all areas of DDI—from research and development to design and implementation—focus on providing integrated, results-oriented products and services that address real-world business needs. Each year more than 12,000 organizations worldwide come to DDI for human resource expertise. These companies include 400 of the *Fortune* 500 in a wide range of businesses—manufacturing, retail, service, and government.

Increasingly, clients are seeking a mix of delivery platforms for their training. DDI has responded by offering CD-ROM-based multimedia for self-study and custom Internet and intranet delivery as well as traditional classroom and paper-and-pencil self-study.

Since its founding in 1970 by industrial psychologists William C. Byham, Ph.D., and Douglas W. Bray, Ph.D., DDI has influenced the work lives of more than 200 million people through its training and consulting services. The company now includes more than 70 offices and affiliates and more than 1,100 employees. DDI's international presence and expertise make it possible for its multinational clients to link hiring, training, and performance management across cultures in 50 countries.

DDI has been a pioneer in several fields. In the '70s the fledgling company introduced the assessment center method—evaluating people based on observation of their behavior in simulations as a predictor of future behavior—to corporate America. On its heels came the first behavior-based interviewing system—Targeted Selection®. As DDI studied existing leadership training and found it provided little or no improvement in job performance, they developed the first commercially available and effective behavior-modeling leadership training system—Interaction Management®. This success led DDI to create dozens of new leadership, team, customer service, and management training products.

- **Change Management**—Implementing a culture that supports the business strategy. This includes senior management strategy sessions, culture change and team consulting, and change management training.

- **Service Culture**—Increasing levels of customer satisfaction and building customer loyalty. The recently redesigned program features culture change consulting, service skills training, and management training support.

- **Leadership and Workforce Development**—Building frontline and middle management leadership talent as well as workforce skills. Assessment, selection, and development areas include leadership, teams, management support, interpersonal skills, and performance management.

- **Selection**—Recruiting and selecting world-class people in an efficient, fair, and legally credible manner. Assessment centers, selection consulting, interviewer training, and computer-based HR systems are among the areas of expertise.

- **Outsourcing**—Allowing a strong focus on core business while reducing overall HR costs. Proven programs and services are assessment and selection, training, interpersonal skill building, executive development, and workforce training.

For more information about the programs and services available from Development Dimensions International, call us between 7:30 a.m. and 5:30 p.m. EST at 1-800-933-4463 in the U.S. or 1-800-668-7971 in Canada.

Also, we would like to hear your reactions to *Organizational Change That Works*. Send your comments to Bob Rogers, COO, Development Dimensions International, World Headquarters—Pittsburgh, 1225 Washington Pike, Bridgeville, PA 15017-2838, or to one of the following e-mail addresses: Internet web site at info@ddiworld.com or the Microsoft® network at ddi@msn.com.

ACKNOWLEDGEMENTS

We would like to thank everyone whose time, effort, and experience are reflected in this book. We'd like to specifically mention *Linda Appel*, editor and project manager for the book; *Andrea Garry* for her astute first-round proof and *Shawn Garry* and *Leslie Patterson* for their more than accurate final proof; *Lynne Weber* for the design and layout; *Mark Mosko* for the graphics found throughout; *Paula Grashoff* for doggedly double-checking references and securing permissions; *Britt Mueller* and *Carla Fogle* for providing research materials; *Elaine Werries* for her copyright expertise; and *William C. Byham, Richard S. Wellins, Alice Pescuric,* and *Bill Jackson* for their feedback and advice.

Many of our clients' stories are in this book, and we would like to thank especially *Jane DeLong*, Vice President of Corporate Resources and Quality Management at Blue Cross and Blue Shield of Montana, and *Jon Woodworth*, Administrative Coordinator of NIBCO Charlestown, for sharing their experiences with the value-driven change process.

Many other client partners helped us put their stories together. We greatly appreciate the efforts of *David Andrews*, Training Manager, Anglian Water; *Barbara Brooks*, Director of Corporate Training and Organization Development, Kemper Insurance Company; *Margot Brown*, Director of External Communications, Motorola, Inc.; *David Christensen*, Associate General Counsel and Assistant Secretary, Carpenter Technology; *Rosemary Chromey*, Director of Human Resources, Sandvik Steel; *Pamela Cook*, Vice President of Human Resources and Best Practices, Mott's USA; *Dorothy Cyr*, Director of Public Affairs, L.L. Bean, Inc.; *Godofredo Deleonardis*, Director of Personnel Relations, Siderca, of Argentina; *Geremy Farmer*, Senior Vice President of Human Resources with First Chicago NBD, and *Diana Kouis; Gale Frazee*, Organization

Development, Buick Motor Division, GMC; *Jeanne Heater*, Vice President, Human Resources, Weiler Corporation; *Farley Houston*, Manager, Employee Relations, ITT-AC Pump; *David Kanally*, Performance Development Initiative, Perot Systems; *Angelle Lafrance*, Staff Support, Organization Design and Development, LaRoche Industries; *Joe Lancaster*, Training Coordinator, Lantech, Inc.; *Sandra Lewis*, Communication Affairs Manager, Miller Brewing Company; *Ruben Nazario*, Vice President, Human Resources, the Milton Hershey School; *Michele R. Papakie*, Chartiers Valley School District Public Relations Coordinator; and *Michael Reusswig*, Vice President of Human Resources, Maytag Cleveland Cooking. A special thanks also to *Beverly Pinzon*, Director of Communications, The Human Resource Planning Society, and *Jerry Probst*, Historian and Archivist, J.C. Penney.

We'd also like to mention the following DDI associates for their contributions: Rick Butler, Dawn Charlier, Karen Colteryahn, Susan Conboy, Jill Faircloth, Tom Falkowski, Michael Foster, Kathy Harper, Maureen Higgins, Connie Hilliard, Tim Jeffrey, Lee Kricher, Helene Lautman, Mike Lehman, Anne Maers, Mike Mariotti, Tracey Moreau, Carrie Mowry, Hallie Pace, Debbie Psihountas, Mark Ralfs, Rick Swegan, and Mary Beth Takacs.

ABOUT THE AUTHORS

Robert W. Rogers

Bob Rogers, chief operating officer (COO) of Development Dimensions International (DDI), manages DDI's North American and European operations. Since becoming COO, he has led the organization through a value-driven change that shifted DDI's culture from one focused on products and sales to one focused on customer and employee retention. Bob's strategic leadership guided the change to redefine DDI's key strategies, drive DDI's values to become meaningful to all associates, reengineer or greatly improve each of DDI's core processes, and expand international operations—all while achieving a compounded annual growth rate of 20 percent during the 1990s. An articulate advocate of having a customer focus, Bob continues to personally work with several key clients each year to stay in touch with the needs of DDI's customers.

Bob has guided or assisted numerous organizations through major organizational changes during his 20 years with DDI. He has performed strategic change work with senior executives from organizations such as Buick Motor Division; Boehringer Ingelheim Pharmaceuticals, Inc.; Cadbury Beverages; Nestle U.K., Ltd.; UCAR Carbon; Warner Lambert; Joy Mining Machinery; Citibank, N.A.; and the Milton Hershey School.

A strong advocate of performance management as the most effective tool to drive strategic change, Bob has helped senior executives in many organizations use performance management to improve organizational focus and success. In this area he has helped clients such as ICI PLC, ICI North America, Georgia-Pacific Corporation, The Allstate Corporation, The Gillette Company, Sonoco Ltd., Norton Healthcare Ltd., and Blue Cross and Blue Shield of Montana.

Bob's expertise extends into DDI's assessment area as well. Originally joining DDI in 1977 as an assessment consultant, he quickly gained recognition in leading DDI's selection and assessment for the Equal Employment Opportunity Commission to select regional directors for the agency's major field offices. He has been involved in major selection and assessment projects for Buick Motor Division, Toyota Motor Corporation, BMW, GTE Corporation, the Federal Trade Commission, the FBI, and many other organizations.

Bob has made presentations at major conferences in the United States, Japan, and the United Kingdom and has written many articles on change, selection, quality service, and performance management. Bob's 1994 monograph, *The Psychological Contract of Trust: Trust Development in the '90s Workplace,* expresses his views on how organizations can best create a corporate culture that dramatically increases the likelihood of success.

John W. Hayden

John Hayden is the vice president of Organizational Change Management at Development Dimensions International. In this capacity he leads a team that provides consulting services in designing, developing, and implementing total, integrated solutions in critical areas such as culture change, organizational needs assessment, strategic planning, high involvement, working in teams, total quality, service quality, and performance management.

John is a specialist in culture-change management. He has worked with leaders in major organizations, such as the Buick Motor Division of General Motors, to establish vision, values, and critical success factors and to design systems that support change efforts. His expertise extends to development of high-involvement infrastructures and the design and implementation of selection systems for facility start-ups.

In his former position as manager of DDI's start-up team, John consulted with organizations to create and implement large-scale assessment and hiring processes for new facilities. He was involved in more than 50 start-up projects, including Libbey Owens Ford Company, Hershey Foods Corporation, Dofasco USA Inc., Benteler Industries, and Welded Tube Company of America. He also worked as a senior account executive with DDI's Eastern Region.

John's work in change consulting and start-ups earned him DDI's President's Award; he also received the company's VIP award four years in succession for consistently surpassing sales objectives in DDI's Eastern Region.

His presentations at professional conferences include "Making Self-Directed Teams Work," "The Empowering Leader," and "Making Self-Managed Quality Work." He has also written articles for professional journals, including *Training, Boardroom Reports,* and *Expansion Management,* on topics that include human resource development, quality, cross-training, and finding and keeping winning employees.

B. Jean Ferketish

Jean Ferketish has worked in organizational change for more than 17 years. In her five years with Development Dimensions International, she created many processes to guide change in organizations, helped clients through the value-driven change process, and implemented self-directed teams. Clients included Dreyer's Grande Ice Cream, the University of Cincinnati Medical Center, Carpenter Technology, and ITT A-C Pump. She also spent 10 years at Westinghouse working in organizational development, quality improvement, and internal communications.

Jean is currently the Director of Organization Development for the University of Pittsburgh. In this role she works with deans and administrators to implement organization effectiveness initiatives with regard to team development, process improvement, and systems alignment.

Jean has written many articles and has been quoted in professional journals on topics such as systems alignment, empowerment, and quality improvement. She speaks frequently on topics including leading change, making change happen and making it work, and organization design for results. She is the 1992 recipient of DDI's President's Award for creating change processes that align the people and process sides of quality improvement. She holds a Ph.D. and an MBA from the University of Pittsburgh.

Robert Matzen

Robert Matzen is the scriptwriter in the Video Productions Department of Development Dimensions International. He has written film and video scripts for all of DDI's major product lines. His videos have earned the New York Film Festival's Gold Medal, the American Corporate Video Crystal Shooting Star, and two CINE Golden Eagle Awards. He has also written videos for the Los Angeles Dodgers Baseball Club; Bally's Health and Tennis Corporation; LaRoche Industries; SEH America, Inc.; Miller Brewing Company; and public television.

At DDI Robert also edited *Empowered Teams* (Jossey-Bass), a book about self-directed work teams written by Richard S. Wellins, William C. Byham, and Jeanne M. Wilson. Before joining DDI, Robert worked as a freelance writer for 11 years. His published materials in that time include the books *Research Made Easy: A Guide for Students and Writers* (Bantam Books) and the Hollywood biography *Carole Lombard* (Greenwood Press) as well as many articles for national magazines.

Other Books from DDI

Select the right people for your organization:

The Selection Solution: Solving the Mystery of Matching People to Jobs by William C. Byham with Steven M. Krauzer

Build an empowered organization:

The Service Leaders Club by William C. Byham with Ray Crew and James H.S. Davis

Zapp!® The Lightning of Empowerment by William C. Byham with Jeff Cox (available on video and audiocassette)

Zapp!® in Education by William C. Byham with Jeff Cox and Kathy Harper Shomo

Zapp!® Empowerment in Health Care by William C. Byham with Jeff Cox and Greg Nelson

HeroZ™—Empower Yourself, Your Coworkers, Your Company by William C. Byham and Jeff Cox (available on audiocassette)

Create and sustain high-performance work teams:

Empowered Teams: Creating Self-Directed Work Groups That Improve Quality, Productivity, and Participation by Richard S. Wellins, William C. Byham, and Jeanne M. Wilson

Inside Teams: How 20 World-Class Organizations Are Winning Through Teamwork by Richard S. Wellins, William C. Byham, and George R. Dixon

Leadership Trapeze: Strategies for Leadership in Team-Based Organizations by Jeanne M. Wilson, Jill George, and Richard S. Wellins, with William C. Byham

Succeeding With Teams: 101 Tips That Really Work by Richard S. Wellins, Dick Schaaf, and Kathy Harper Shomo

Team Leader's Survival Guide by Jeanne M. Wilson and Jill A. George

Team Member's Survival Guide by Jill A. George and Jeanne M. Wilson

Understand how Japanese companies operate outside Japan:

Shogun Management™: How North Americans Can Thrive in Japanese Companies by William C. Byham with George Dixon

And new for DDI:

Landing the Job You Want: How to Have the Best Job Interview of Your Life by William C. Byham with Debra Pickett

INDEX

☆ ☆ ☆

culture, organizational, 11–15, 119;
altering existing culture, 12, 14;
defined, 11; and ethics
(Sundstrand), 13–14; impact on
business strategy, 15; lack of
culture guidance (Sundstrand),
13–14, 17; management of, 84;
role in change, 11–15; and
strategic focus, 55–56; tied to
productivity and profitability,
12–13, 14

D

Deming, Dr. W. Edwards, 29, 98
Development Dimensions
International, 22, 74, 80, 104
Dillon, John T., and International
Paper Company, 72
dimensions/competencies, 80, 83
driving value, 48

E

Eichinger, Robert, 5
environmental scans, 39–40

F

facilitating values, 48
Federal Express, 43, 45, 52, 79
Fifth Discipline, The, 29–30
First Chicago NBD, 105–106
Fisher, George, and Kodak, 79

G

Galvin, Robert, and Motorola,
68–69
General Electric, and Jack Welch,
45, 72, 79
General Motors and Saturn, 45
Gilmartin, Ray, and Merck and Co.,
Inc., 79
grapevine, 72–73
Great Game of Business, The, 112
Guzzo, Richard A., 45–46

H

health care and the value-driven
change process, 142
Hershey, Milton, School, 78
Heskett, James, 12
Hewlett-Packard, 45
high-involvement change strategy,
19–20; defined, 19
horizontal organizational structure,
86–89
Human Resource Planning Society,
5–7

I

In the Age of the Smart Machine, 85
information management systems,
106–107, 118
insurance industry, 5
International Business Machines
(IBM), 45
International Paper Company, and
John T. Dillon, 72
ITT A-C Pump, 39

J

job design, 84–85
job rotation systems, 107
Johnson & Johnson and Tylenol, 43

K

Kaplan, Robert S., 18
Kemper Insurance Company, 93–94
Kennedy, John F., and the new
frontier, 24, 32, 35, 63–64, 125
Kodak, and George Fisher, 79
Kotter, John, 12, 15, 79

L

lag indicators, 17, 78
Lantech, Inc., 95
Larkin, Sandar, 51, 119
Larkin, T.J., 51, 119
LaRoche Industries Inc., 67, 128–129
Lawler, Edward III, 79, 84
lead indicators, 17, 78
learning tension, 91
Louis, Meryl Reis, 12, 15, 19